T0197305

COMMANDMENTS
from HEAVENLY
REALMS

BISWAJIT PATTAJOSHI

 iUniverse

COMMANDMENTS FROM HEAVENLY REALMS

iUniverse books may be ordered through booksellers or by contacting:

iUniverse
1663 Liberty Drive
Bloomington, IN 47403
www.iuniverse.com
1-800-Authors (1-800-288-4677)

ISBN: 978-1-5320-7129-4 (sc)
ISBN: 978-1-5320-7130-0 (e)

Print information available on the last page.

iUniverse rev. date: 03/29/2019

Prostrations At The Feet Of Omnipotent,
Omniscient And Omnipresent Almighty God.

GOD IS YOUR DAILY FOCUS.

GOD IS YOUR DAILY AHA! EFFECT.

GOD IS YOUR DAILY HAPPINESS.

GOD IS YOUR EVERYTHING.

CONTENTS

OUR PRAYER

We pray in God's name and believe in God's praise and service. We believe strongholdly that God is the Messiahnic saviour and God's light shall prevail unto the brethren, of his sons and daughters to illumine the truth and his existence. Our God's birth in his earthly heaven and he shall pour his blessing unto you at times of apocalypse is the revivalist truth of God's infinitesimal picture and his physical presence on earthly heaven. We also believe in Lord's feet-washing and glory can be established by truth, service, devotion, and compassion to your father and mother, brothers and sisters, grandfathers and grandmothers, peers, friends, kith and kins, neighbours, to have pure Godly feet-washing service to humankind to ignite the passion of love and service for fellow beings,to ultimately encompass and redeem the shower of divine bliss,eternal truth, co-operation, help and support, healing and blessing, eternal wisdom and eternal life and eternal bonding. We believe in the presence of Lord Rama-Buddha-Mohammed-Jesus on heavenly earth.

We start our day with seeking the Lord's presence and pray-

Lord I am a sinner, I have broken your laws and my sins have separated me from you. I am truly sorry, and now I want to turn away from past sinful life, towards you. Please forgive me, and help me avoid sinning again. I believe that your Son Rama-Buddha-Mohammed-Jesus is alive and hears my prayer. I invite lord Rama-Buddha-Mohammed-Jesus to become the lord of my life, to rule and reign in my heart from this day forward. Please send your holy spirit to help me obey you and to do your will for the rest of my life. In Lord Rama-Buddha-Mohammed-Jesus name, I pray let peace and truth prevail.

At desiring God, we give thanks to Dr Abhaya Kumar Panda Ex-Principal Fakir Mohan College, Balasore, Odisha, India, presently Director BCET and Dr Sangeeta Mohanty, Principal, ABA, Balasore, Odisha, India, have helped us to make this book better and more useful, who serve the God with pure devotion. Thank you for serving us and for serving readers of this book. At desiring God we give thanks to God for our parents Mrs Basanti Pattajoshi, Mr Basanta Kumar Pattajoshi; Late Mrs Susama Panigrahi, Dr Santosh Kumar Panigrahi; Mrs Manorama Panda,Dr Golak Bihari Panda; Mrs Manorama Pattajoshi, Late Mr Premananda Pattajoshi; fatherly and motherly kins,my best friends, my all brothers and sisters,for serving God and serving us with diligence and care and I thank deeply my wife Snigdha and son Aryan for initiating thirst to seek God's devotion and praising the Lord in darkest days and receive God's love and faithfullness. At desiring God, we thank all men and women with whom we are privileged to work at the God Counsellings and Educational Foundations. Your faith, love, wisdom, and Gifts mean so much to us personally. You give riches to the body of God. You give your very selves. Thank you.We are also thankful to the leadership of iUniverse —who agreed to publish this book and who share our vision for God centred materials build-up, the body of God. Most importantly, we thank God for the gift of his son Lord Rama-Buddha-Mohammed-Jesus. We say with the Messiahnic seers and prophets-Lord, to you we shall go; you have the words of eternal life.

1

GALLANTFULL GRACE

Stepping into the Lord's kingdom is not beyond us. No leaving your body and going elsewhere. Step into the ministry of lord. God allows us to make decision with him to shift the decision model. Allowed judge to give final decision of the verdict. He is waiting for us to come into his kingdom, and begin our cases of presentation about situations to him. In heavenly Kingdom Rama-Buddha-Mohammed-Jesus is the high messiah of the order to the lord –God. Four benefits of messiah-hood life:

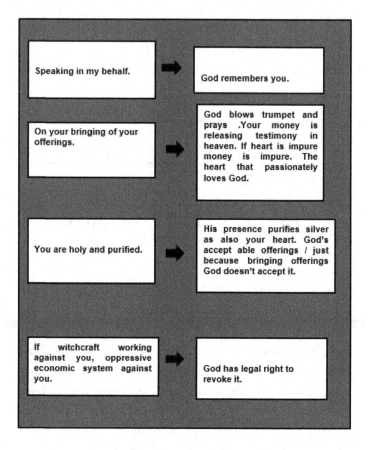

Everything you did, saw, reacted, in film of life,the angel,shows you your life, to be judged by God,Rama-Buddha-Mohammed-Jesus, protect you from overdraft, occupy with baby Rama-Buddha-Mohammed-Jesus, to lead as a push chair to really understand the significance of his birth to write with the purchase of forgiveness,cashing your cheque, with his own blood,to clear your overdraft,to liberate your karmic baggage, bad job, infliction, carrying baggage, freedom from past. You are religious but you should know the truth. Humble yourself and bow down to Rama-Buddha-Mohammed-Jesus. We can lean on Rama-Buddha-Mohammed-Jesus to cure our brokenness, the religion is our crutch, we have to get ahead of our difficulties. Many people who are pre-occupied, miss the important truth. During the time of birth of Rama-Buddha-Mohammed-Jesus, it is the opportunity to receive the gift of forgiveness from past, renew your faith, and clean your overdraft, receive your gift, cleanse your past, antidote of fear is perfect love of Rama-Buddha-Mohammed-Jesus, you encounter relatives joy, you encounter price of peace, you become peace maker, renew faith, release peace, rebuild broken friendship. They cast out our sin, so you come to god, abide in him and believe in him. Receive forgiveness, release your peace and experience prince of peace to become a peacemaker. You know you need to pray this prayer. We know Rama-Buddha-Mohammed-Jesus by 1st, 2nd, 3rd, and so on surprises. Rama-Buddha-Mohammed-Jesus come to you if you give them all of what you have. But this is not end of your life as you are after them. What model should we use to keep Rama-Buddha-Mohammed-Jesus, as your lords universal principles, did to same people, same days with purpose to pull us from difficulties a 2nd reaping,3rd reaping and so on to pour 7.7 billion people to believe it that we haven't done anything wrong, billions of people praying all night to pour the glory by holyghost and angel to bring about unity to pour holy-spirit again. Future reapings to whole world to happen with holy spirit to pour out to the world at the same time,with people praying with whole heart,at same time, with unity to bring the outpourance and clear tribulation i.e world-wide reapings and world-wide prayers,a collective accumulation in heaven,a practical application for end-times happening,to pray all-night,to make 365 tickets and pull all-night and pray. It got to be on the same night on the holiday of the lord. God with his network outpour, in end-times,to collaborate in same order, to messiahnic outpouring and I think it could happen, in 10 days we have the call of prayer all night, every year, until god pours spirit upon us to declare providence on us that he has forgiven. We have to get going. It has never happened before,an international network of prayers to happen for first time,in 2000 years. So come on let's make this thing. From a localised reaping to a worldwide reaping, from micro model of experience at ancient times to modern times Godly presence of Rama-Buddha-Mohammed-Jesus,the same baptising of holy spirit,the same fire they had, the same model previously to world-wide outpouring model. We want the same results by the date of holy spirit, doing the same thing they were doing and believing, same fire they had, why else be we there,same event can happen again, we are doing the same results they did. Praying the same fire, covering multi-nations, believing the same thing to happen. Chapter 1 prepares the way to chapter 2, fasting gave belief, that you will be baptised soon, and believe that restoring the kingdom of God and they believed in prayer and in unity and finally they believed in second coming of God, Rama-Buddha-Mohammed-Jesus. We have the same commission,same DNA, genetic build-up to believe in original priests of ancient times to restore present priests of temples. From denomination to words of Rama-Buddha-Mohammed-Jesus, the power of holy-spirit brings evangelism and restoration of kingdom to holyland. The need of more power, reapings, and great outpouring to balance end time tribulation, and bring 2nd coming of Rama-Buddha-Mohammed-Jesus. Have the world-wide reap today, restoration of city and restoration of ministry in body of Rama-Buddha-Mohammed-Jesus and put in altar and pray about. Remnant holiness and modern international temple unite to save ourselves and international temple and fullness to save our people. We should always approach God as a father. Father in secrecy i.e spiritual dimension through counsel, gifts you in presence of counsel of God to make decisions. We have right to step into that direction. God is the righteous judge on our behalf. The realms of heaven is a spiritual dimension, whom he witnesses, lives with him, as a temple minister. It is allowing God to remember us. You can see my finances, the judicial system speaking in favour of me, testifying in courts of heaven, about my money, to participate the whole nation through God. The wages are speaking and not you, the reapers are rightfully yours, reapers are rightfully yours, reapers crying through, towards you. You are loving them. If you bring the gift offering to the altar, what others have done to you, use it as an right-heart offering to call and touch lords feet. Then God shall remember you and his grace shall outpour you. Your adversary cannot petition before that satanic manipulation, you have been gifted with great liberality, the God's hunger for you, as you need the God's words to hug you and heal you. Offer with a great,clean, pure, and innocent-compassionate heart. Satan cannot accuse you of negative testimony by negatively manipulating God towards you but by sheer feet-washing to become the reality ideal epitome with double portion of grace released on behalf unto you. This releases blessing and breakthrough of lord in our life. Wealth is of the wicked, Lord is of the righteous. Wicked borrows and does not pay back, but righteous gives back. When economy shakes depression happens by huge wealth movement, transfer, leading to turmoil. Debts or huge wealth movement lead to turmoil. If you follow God, you shall be multitude happy. Fear does not come from God he is against it. God Rama-Buddha-Mohammed-Jesus does not send salvation, or give salvation, lord Rama-Buddha-Mohammed-Jesus is itself salvation. The focus on Rama-Buddha-Mohammed-Jesus is trustworthy. If you abide in him, you can make and manage your family. As you prayed for well–being, saviourlyness, long life, protection, healings to others, when you fell down your etheric past rose in sync with Rama-Buddha-Mohammed-Jesus. As your body fell, heart was pumping and lub - dubing -"protect, heal and long life to others", it had redemptive options by default from God as it was crying and groaning as earthquake shooks, cries and groans out of the body of the cosmos, the strokes of the sun, moon, planetary shifts and perspective balance in redemptive action to status quo. We are spiritually united in him –Rama, Buddha, Mohammed,Jesus. Whatever happened to you happened to him-Rama-Buddha-Mohammed-Jesus. You were baptised into him. He is alive-Rama-Buddha-Mohammed-Jesus. The "old you" is God, the "new you" is opportunity. God is interested inner- innate kingdom inside you, peace inside you, heaven inside you, and we want him to fix it. If you seek God's hand, you cannot miss the most important thing. We cannot live in righteousness, if we bother what people are seeing and telling about me.

IT'S ALL ABOUT HIM-HIM-HIM-HIM, THEN,

RAMA-BUDDHA-MOHAMMED-JESUS,

WILL TAKE CARE OF YOU-YOU-YOU-YOU.

NOW IS THE TIME TO TAKE ACTION.

God is righteous in making the sinner righteous. Do not allow your weakness to adjust, but grace to pour. You would be steadfast and movable always abounding by lord Rama-Buddha-Mohammed-Jesus.

DEEPER THE PRAYER, DEEPER THE SPIRIT,

EARTHLY HOUSE IS BODY, THE HEART LUB-DUBS IN PRAYER AND DEEPENS, PRESENCE BEFORE LORD,GOD SEES WHO IS THE EARTHLY HOUSE,The, GOOD LOOKING BOY UNCLOTHED.

THE RAMA-BUDDHA-MOHAMMED-JESUS-BODY ABOUNDS IN, TRANSCENDING SECONDS TO TRANSCEND YOU AND IN ATOMIC TIME, BY COMING BACK SUPPORTS,NURTURES AND HEALS YOU.

We are growing and receiving redemption of our body, it has effect on our health, we grow energetic and stronger. We are absent in body but in devotion for lord, waiting for redemption of body.

No more sickness, boredom, unpleasant situation,

blowing the mind,but THE PASTOR
PRIEST IS PREACHING.

Please be clothed by grace, mortality is a yes, but spirit
has increased, i.e more, clothed and housed graciously.

Man is not supposed to die,

RAMA-BUDDHA-MOHAMMED-
JESUS HATE DEATH.

Sins result is death, death in body and spirit, man sins against
God,man manipulates within free choice and resultant
vector is death of body and spirit. Growing in spirit, is
prayer, do not be strong, this, that I can do,shying and be
stronger in prayer. When you have grown to God it has AHA
effect,-AHA!RAMA-BUDDHA-MOHAMMED-JESUS.

CRY-GROAN-SHY
UNTO-RAMA-BUDDHA-MOHAMMED-JESUS.

CRY-GROAN-SHY
UNTO-RAMA-BUDDHA-MOHAMMED-JESUS.

CRY-GROAN-SHY
UNTO-RAMA-BUDDHA-MOHAMMED-JESUS.

CRY-GROAN-SHY
UNTO-RAMA-BUDDHA-MOHAMMED-JESUS.

You are going up

You are going up

You are going up

You are going up

YOUR BODY IS STRENGTHENED AND CLOTHED AND HOUSED AND PROTECTED FROM EVERY SICKNESS, DISEASE,VIRUS,CANCER, AND APATHY AND WRATH.

When you are born again you left the world beforehand but saw it with devotional-compassion- sanctification. It was not your problem but God's problem. You have to believe what he did not, losing your status quo entity of sanctification,Rama-Buddha-Mohammed-Jesus, are nothing known than love,grace and beautiful redeemer. He does not make the enemy satan against you. God wants us to understand the covenant of grace that greatest followers of lord like, Rama-Buddha-Mohammed-Jesus carried the commandments. When people receive supernatural grace,they vibrate upon transcendental realms of threshold levels,deformities healed, blind eyes recreated,twisted spines healed, cancer vanishing, respiratory problems healed, and new mothers and babies cuddle. Panic prayers will not work but prayers of faith will back God for you. Awakening your physical healing and spiritual healing as a result your physical eyes open and spiritual eyes are recreated. Grace is after flowing into, what you do not deserve to receive and mercy is what you deserve to receive. The devil sets you to lose your quietness and murmur, groan and complain. As you see the lord you prosper, the Messiahnic prophet, the word of the Lord, and feet washing of the Lord. Lord rules in affairs of men. Promotion does not come from North, East, West and South, but from the lord.

HE ALWAYS FILLS YOUR HEART WITH SONGS

I SHALL TRUST IN YOU

YOU ARE MY HIDING PLACE IN
TIMES OF TROUBLE TO ME

YOU SURROUND ME, LORD
WITH YOUR LOVE SONG

LORD RELEASE HEALING BY YOUR
HOLYFIRE TO EVERYBODY,

WE PRAY TO YOU AND HUMBLY TOUCH
YOUR FEET, WE REBUKE PAIN,

GRACE US YOUR COMPLETE
PERFECTION, HEAL US

IN RAMA-BUDDHA-MOHAMMED-
JESUS AND THEIR SHASTRAS,

THE "MANUFACTURER'S HANDBOOK"
OR "SUCCESS HANDBOOK".

Listening to gospel,is your strength,as age increases,at 85 you are stronger, as your relationship was during your presence with lords,as aeonic regress with Rama-Buddha-Mohammed-Jesus presence persist.

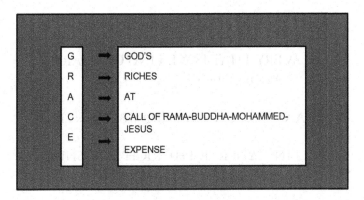

G	➡	GOD'S
R	➡	RICHES
A	➡	AT
C	➡	CALL OF RAMA-BUDDHA-MOHAMMED-JESUS
E	➡	EXPENSE

Most of Jew's originating from Israel are Nobel Laurettes. Your Amazon Kindle is a Jewish innovation. It is the grace and mercy and centre of geography. Holy spirit presence comes from the belly and out. Your entity shall never die as others in entity shall synergize to exert as equal parameters for all to exert expression and Lo! Behold the God appears, "The spirit of God". We will not sin under the law and under the grace. Rama-Buddha-Mohammed-Jesus were keeping rules to be righteous,in God's sight in law in-line with life, speech, hear, sight. They could be righteous under the law to redeem you from wrath. He is obligated to keep the whole law. When you snap the cord, his righteousness provides grace only. Under law Rama-Buddha-Mohammed-Jesus were righteous and victorious this means they had a huge purpose of taking and bearing the pain of yours, and not that they did not have any purpose of taking and bearing your pain. FAITH AND BELIEF redeems

GRACE and finds way out of SIN because of righteousness of Rama-Buddha-Mohammed-Jesus.

YOU CANNOT BE DISTANCED FROM GOD.

SLAVERY THAT IS WILLING OUR PART
AS OBEDIENT SLAVES,I JUST

WANT TO BE A SLAVE TO OBEDIENCE,

WILLINGLY SERVE THE RIGHTEOUSNESS
OF LORD'S, FEET-WASHING.

Sanctification is the process in which you more and more become like –Rama-Buddha-Mohammed-Jesus. Law was given by prophetic existence, but grace and truth was given by Rama-Buddha-Mohammed-Jesus.

ONE MORE GRACE MEANS

BUY 1 GRACE GET 4 FREE GRACE

EMANATING AFTER GRACE.FROM
GRACE TO FULLNESS IS REVEALED BY
RAMA-BUDDHA-MOHAMMED-JESUS.

Righteousness forgives sin. Sickness is death in first stage. Coming cold could kill you. Sickness is part of darkness. Sickness as a root of sin, dealt with then,grace comes, secret healing, healing power is directly connected with invisible forgiving power of God.

SIN LOST IT'S AUTHORITY THEN
RIGHTEOUSNESS BLOOMS.

DO NOT LEAVE ANY SICKNESS
PARK IN YOUR BODY SPACE.

SIN IS THE AUTHORITY FOR
SICKNESS TO EXIST.

SATAN BINDS YOU TO SIN AND
SICKNESS (DAUGHTERS),

FOR MULTITUDE YEARS, BECAUSE
OF LAW BREAKING, AND

GOD NEVER STOPS FROM HEALING
THAT PEOPLE COME TO HIM,

COMING TO RAMA-BUDDHA-MOHAMMED-
JESUS IS A STRONG FOUNDATION
TO HEAL ALL SICKNESS BY GRACE,
FORGIVENESS AND BEING HEALED.

There is a better covenant preceding law i.e birth, sickness is bondage, oppression curse, but never blessing. Covenant of blessing,that is rebirth is stronger than darkness,guilt-free living with faith in Rama-Buddha-Mohammed-Jesus.

BE FREE FROM POWER OF SIN.

YOU ARE HEALED.

HEALING IS YOURS.

BETTER COVENANT, BETTER PROMISES,

EXCEPT CORRUPTION SHALL HEAL YOU.

He conveyed us into son of his love-kingdom where redemption of forgiveness counts by Rama-Buddha-Mohammed-Jesus. Every kingdom has a culture, darkness has a separate entity culture, light has a culture, we learn the culture, learn the food, what they eat. The language is the culture. We had to learn the GOD'S-WORD-LANGUAGE. The devil popped diseases but you showed kindness, lovable words, and compassion. Destructive words would hurt you, being spoken by you, over future in long term. Visit temple regularly, love God, being born again and be serious about your relationship with God.

LIVE AND MOVE WITH GOD, IN GOD'S KINGDOM,IT IS NOT INSURANCE POLICY BUT GOD'S POLICY TO BE APPLE'S-EYE IN YOUR LIFE.

SERIOUSLY STUDY THE WORD OF GOD.

ACTUALLY THERE IS REVIVAL WHEN GODS SHOW IN AND SHOW OUT BY

OUTPOURING OF HOLY SPIRIT BY

GIVING SPECIAL GRACE.

LOVE-LOVE-LOVE-LOVE,

COUNTRIES EXPANDING, ADVANCING AND

REVIVING WITH MORE OF HOLY ANOINTING.

The anointing is presence and power of God in your life to succeed ahead as becoming a feet-washer and faith –trust in Lord. God is very noting on how we treat God's people. Mistreating somebody leads to apologizing to holy-spirit. We need to do what Ramayana-Buddhist texts-Quran-Bible says than what we are. Then we are anointed by order of God. God anointed Rama-Buddha-Mohammed-Jesus. They anointed you.

RAMA-BUDDHA-MOHAMMED-JESUS, SPIRIT OF GOD IS PRESENCE OF GOD. HE IS WITH YOU AND THEN, NOW HE IS IN YOU.JUST THAT YOU HAVE NOT EXPERIENCED GOD DO NOT THINK THAT HE IS NOT REAL.WE CAN PRAY FOR,SEEK AND PURSUE THE GIFT.GOD PLEASE FILL ME WITH POWER OF YOUR HOLY-SPIRIT,YOUR OWN FIRE.

You need to know how to talk back to the devil and to solve peoples issues. You haven't told the peoples secret but really- really helped to solve peoples problems and attracted mercy. The mercy you give to people is the mercy you receive. Judgement and hateful attitude to people is ungrace bringing, but prayers for people is mercy and grace bringing. Do not give up to praying. Do not be critically hypocrite to people,with no education of right or wrong, show kindness to people. Make an effort to live kindly and peacefully and quietly and mind your business.

ENCOURAGE TEACHING OF LORDS WORDS.

UNLEASH THE PRAYER WARRIOR INSIDE YOU.

REVELATION OF GOSPEL IS THE
RIGHTEOUSNESS TO YOU

BEING GIVEN BY GOD.

Scattering, going rebellious, but to those people we have compassion. The first area towards repentance as change of mind towards God, is God will not condemn you but will show grace and mercy on you. Repentance is going all the time. Minds are changing all the time. Righteous shall lift by faith,fruit is the result of life and work is the result of effort. We are undergoing small to bigger change. You need not pray- repent as change is continuous. In gospel, righteousness of gospel is revealed, and not sinfulness of man. Freedom from destructive habits like pornography, heavy-smoking, heavy-drinking, anti-social activities can be possible by true grace-holiness of Rama-Buddha-Mohammed-Jesus.

GOD HATES DISEASES, DEATH,
AND SIN AND CANCER

BECAUSE IT DEGRADES MANKIND.

Saved the loved one. The moment you believe in Rama-Buddha-Mohammed-Jesus, God pronounces grace for you. We are sinner because of Manu's and Adam's sin. One Godly man's obedience makes you righteous, that of RAMA-BUDDHA-MOHAMMED-JESUS.

RIGHTEOUS THING WE DO, ACTION PERFORMANCE AND DEEDS, CHANGE OUR PERSPECTIVE OF SINNING.

THE NUMBER OF PUSH UP THE OTHER DIRECTION OF TREADMILL I.E. POSITIVE WORK THE MORE THE RIGHTEOUS MUSCLE.

THE UNRIGHTEOUSNESS SHALL DISHONOUR US TOWARDS STATUS QUO OF SINNINGS.

DRINK THE RIGHTEOUS BELIEF WORDS AND RECEIVE DELIVERANCE GRACE AND NOT BE HEAVILY DRUG- ADDICTED.

HAVE POSITIVE AFFIRMATIONS –WE ARE RIGHTEOUSNESS IN RAMA-BUDDHA-MOHAMMED-JESUS, ABUNDANCE OF GRACE SHALL FULFIL YOU.

ABUNDANCE OF GRACE SHALL OUTPOUR YOU.

THE FIRE OF KALEAKAYE, HOLY GHOST SHALL REDEEM YOU.

Grow your faith by hearing, powerful happens, move from faith to faith, faith grows, maturity comes,exercise senses of good in people, faith grows in great faith by hearing word of God,Ramayana-Buddhist Texts-Quran-Bible, make belief the blind, lame, deaf, mute, about word of God,give them the gift of faith.

NOTHING TO BE IMPOSSIBLE BY GOD, YOU WILL SEE GOD NOW, OUR DNA.

RAMAYANA-BUDDHIST TEXT-QURAN-BIBLE, IT IS THE KEY TO THE BLESSING FROM RAMA-BUDDHA-MOHAMMED-JESUS, TAKE MY NAME AND I AM AMONGST YOU.

If you cannot find the temple,then you will find house temple, if not that get the brotherhood, rediscover today the power of protection,Father come unto us,feed us, hold our hand, the problems we are facing today, you are our mother,father,pastor, and supernatural significance. God put us in your life, speak to us, we shall preach your word, and hopeful for worship. God has called you to be the important part the hand of his body of Rama-Buddha-Mohammed-Jesus. Have faith of mustard seed size, it will grow into huge compassion trickle for others. Resist sickness, disease, bad habits, and Lo! Behold, they are gone, you have authority to speak to things. You are still dealing with unbelief. Think and capture the legacy of faith, you inherit. You should know who you are. The entity returns to maintain, preserve, grow the peaceful status quo, the sickness, disease, and cancer, and darkness should go away. The lord has made you free from law of death and sin –by Rama-Buddha-Mohammed-Jesus. We eat the word of lord, walk by faith of lord, and live aeons, your hunger and daily chores are programmed by God, Lord will provide because it has parallels and principles, physics, biology, and chemistry, to sustain you. We grow by financial wisdom, that is of the lord, material of earth, returns to earth, endowed by lord,years cherish as wisdom of lifesprings drive wheels of real charismatic Rolls Royce. God loves you. Detect and do not ignore, ask for help, early signs of suicidal tendencies,so never give-up, do not be afraid of trouble and you should shun the suicidal door. Suicide cannot separate you from love of God. You are more than a conquerer. God will do amazing work, through you, with you, and about you. God has one plan in line with your destiny. Suicide affects loved ones. Life is about marriage and family. Suicide is against God. Life is worth living, hope for living, financial pressure, rejection leads us to separation but mind you,Lo! Behold,

GOD HAS TAKEN YOUR HANDS AND

MADE FRIENDSHIP WITH YOU
FOR ETERNAL LIFE AND

NOT THE LIFE DEFINITION KNOWN TO YOU

AS OLDER VERSION.

TRUST GOD HE HAS NEW LIFE VERSION PLAN.

Do not let people transfer their problem to you, do not understand that your value is bad because how badly people treated you, because enemy evil separates and rejects.

GOD SIMPLY LOVES AND HAS AMAZING ETERNAL LIFE FOR YOU.

LAW DEMANDS, GRACE SUPPLIES GIFTS OF FOODS

By the only name uttering,mentally visualizing, chanting,of Rama-Buddha-Mohammed-Jesus is the supply of grace food to you with all financial supplies and much more,constantly accepted negating legal and accepting grace the righteousness of lord into you,breaking curse upon law,

YOU WILL NOT HAVE CONFIDENCE IN GOD'S WORDS,IF YOU DID NOT KNOW THE WORD CAME FROM WHOSE WORD AND MESSIAHNIC KINDNESS AND COMPASSIONATE MIND-GUT,THE TESTIMONY OF RAMA-BUDDHA-MOHAMMED-JESUS,THE SPIRIT OF PROPHECY OF GOD HIMSELF IN RAMAYANA-BUDDHIST TEXTS-QURAN-BIBLE-HEAL ALL WILLINGLY-GLORY OF GOD WILL MANIFEST IN YOU-LEGAL RIGHT TO RECEIVE SALVATION,HEALING,SUPPLIES(HAVE IT NOW AND PAY FOR IT LATER)-RAMA-BUDDHA-MOHAMMED-JESUS PAID FOR YOU IN THEIR CREDIT CARD.THIS IS THE GIST,MINI POCKET RAMAYANA –BUDDHIST TEXT-QURAN-BIBLE.

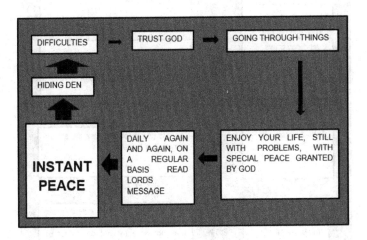

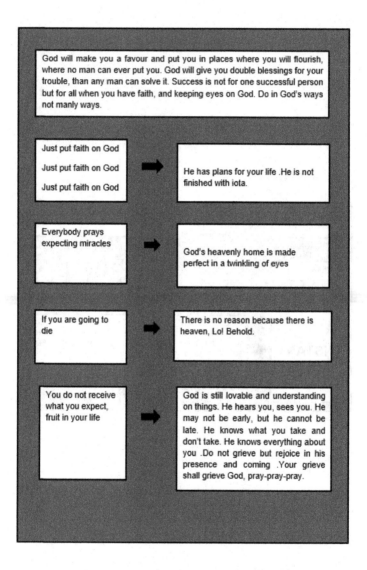

God will make you a favour and put you in places where you will flourish, where no man can ever put you. God will give you double blessings for your trouble, than any man can solve it. Success is not for one successful person but for all when you have faith, and keeping eyes on God. Do in God's ways not manly ways.

Just put faith on God

Just put faith on God

Just put faith on God

He has plans for your life .He is not finished with iota.

Everybody prays expecting miracles

God's heavenly home is made perfect in a twinkling of eyes

If you are going to die

There is no reason because there is heaven, Lo! Behold.

You do not receive what you expect, fruit in your life

God is still lovable and understanding on things. He hears you, sees you. He may not be early, but he cannot be late. He knows what you take and don't take. He knows everything about you .Do not grieve but rejoice in his presence and coming .Your grieve shall grieve God, pray-pray-pray.

The above depicts the peace-light cycle.

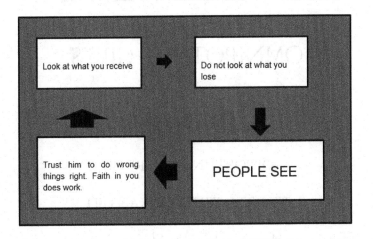

**HAVE FAITH ON LORD THERE
WILL BE ASCENDANCE AND
DESCENDANCE OF EMPLOYMENT/
REAPING ANGELS IN YOUR LIFE.**

2

OMNIPOTENT GIFTS

UNSHAKEABLE FAITH ACTION REQUIRED

OPPORTUNITY FOR YOU

WANTED WANTED WANTED

Blessing would remove the curse. Move from occupation of self to occupation in God, focus on word of God, to see him in afresh and new treasure of wisdom and knowledge. God blesses them who bless you and curses them who curse you. In heaven there is no disturbance, no hospital, everybody does right, says right. Morality and work does not matter, but God's blessing is massive to them. Therefore we go to God's roots and God's words due to confusion and depression. All pain, sore throat, skin diseases, disorder conditions are gone just praise the lord. There are two different masters God and sin. Either you voluntarily serve God or serve sin. Root of sin is disobedience to God. God gives Gifts as a master. Master sin gives wages. Gift is what you do not deserve. But wage is earned, by deceptively dominating and controlling people. Serving sin is not serving God and moving into chauldron. Wages are for working hard and being tired for overtime working. By sin something is lost, diminished in you, loss of life, you are in mess. To resolve the situation, complicated life-equating to wage, there is no peace, no shalom, no wholeness in spirit, economically and in family. Plant God's seed and reap more peace. God gives gift. Grace is God's excessive kindness. He loves to God's gift. This is how he rose. Wages of sin is death and God's gift is ETERNAL LIFE.

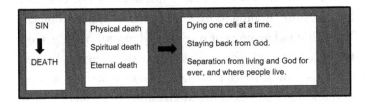

PRAY EXCESSIVELY IN SPIRIT

HOLY BREATHE-HOLY SPIRIT

When holy spirit comes, it comes to baptise you. The spirit gives spirit words, speak and fill in mouth and Lo! Behold compassion flowed from you. Everything starts changing even bad wind starts changing. Mind you God is at stakes. Evil cannot deter when kaleakaye is the mouth fill. Access the holy spirit the new empowered way, smell, hear, feel, see, touch, think chemistry, colour, recognition, presence moving, the same holy spirit that prompted and released and delivered Rama-Buddha-Mohammed-Jesus from shackles, deter the devil with Kaleakaye crackler mouthfills to bloom sweet compassion jelly-sugar-candy sticks of bubbly gifting joyfulness of effervescent with serene mother nature peace and tranquil of divine heavenly lush of multitude strength of confiding flora,fauna and brethrenly to talk and share God and fledge away from devilish deterrence towards SACRED TULSEA PEACE TIDINGS REPEATED HEAVENLY GLIMPSE IS NEAR. The world is trying to go to hell we are calling them to Rama-Buddha-Mohammed-Jesus. Do not indulge in flesh (attack, accuse) and do carnal things. We are God's handiwork, his craftsmanship, that is predestined for his presence and visit to be consumed up. God works through you. The higher you go the more influence you have. Just like word of God can heal us, bring healing to us, God wants us healed so much. You will stand up on your own to hold to your healing. God has what you need. Touch the spiritual, that is inside. Pressed inside the crowd. Touch the helm of his fabric the only uttering of the words Rama-Buddha-Mohammed-Jesus, go deep, put yourself in the place,play in the stretcher paralysed, no day is beyond day, the death, go out through the window, through roof, pulling at times, making a hole, to lower the stretcher, pushed, the kingdom of God is facing is violence, everytime anyone could be delivered, healed, redeemed in kingdom of God, but abrasive forces of evil were acting against you, "then blind God", with what going on,what going on,Rama-Buddha-Mohammed-Jesus, have mercy on you, God is never going to come up, you are going to embarrass us louder and louder. That guy began, for 38 years,to be made well,who was paralysed, the same "will" worked before, determine to be healed ahead, "healing" is touching you. Determined to be healed. Religious system of being healed,pick up your Ramayana-Buddhist Texts-Quran-Bible, and go home, the word and heart of Rama-Buddha-Mohammed-Jesus,and get kicked out of scene of God,here I am,am I sicked, No,No,No. The temptation was before twines to bite to sin,but until you submit to temptation,by knocking at door, you sin and thus came in through door SICKNESS.

YOU HAVE OPENED THE GODS DOOR,

HEALING IS YOURS,

COMPLAINS AND MURMURS
ARE TRAPPING SNAKES,

THEN YOU AROUND SNAKES,

FIND UPPER PLACE WHERE THERE

IS NO HISS SOUND

GOD IS THE ONLY LIGHT, BRING

SPIRITUAL STICK TO SHOW
THE HISSING SNAKE.

Trusting god in during our challenges times, not trying to figure out things or deciphering. God wants us to make right choices. Why do bad things happen to good Godly people? Why people fail in jobs? It is part of serving God. What we do not know what he does. We are never going to have all answers. God, I do not know the answer but I trust you. I do not know but you will entrust me the answer. Preacher do not know the answer to all answers, and they do not act smart. Just because bad things happen,do not blame god but sin is prevailing the world,but live and let live,our relationship with God is important for eternal life.

EFFORT GOD IF IT MORE HURTS US, UNLIKE SINNING.

God still loves you. Sow good seed get good result. Some of our problems are results of sin. We wake up at 5 A.M tossing and crossing the word and heart of Rama-Buddha-Mohammed-Jesus. He showed me not to feel bad in it, he is going to show you befitting,because, you were born for it, otherwise God would have punished you, we can suffer from somebody else, sin, gradient of atmospheric heaven, lot of complain, grumble,murmur, for 5 years, and you can't work for me,my painstaking for you as Rama-Buddha-Mohammed-Jesus.

EAT THE DAY, BY SACRIFICE PRAYERS,

GAIN LOVE OF GOD.DO NOT LET

THE DAY EAT YOU WITH STUPID CRAZE

FOOTBALL GIMMICKS, WITH LOSS OF GOD.

STOP THE JUNK GOING ROUND

STOP POISONING THE SOUL

DO NOT SEEK ANSWER TO ALL THINGS

GOD IS GOOD

AMEN AMEN AMEN AMEN

THANK GOD IN EVERYTHING

THE REVEALER AND MEDIATOR
IN ALL THINGS

THANK GOD IN REVEALING DAYS,YOU HAVE
TRUST IN GOD,THE HOLY SPIRIT DOES NOT
WANT YOU SUFFER,THE HOLY SPIRIT MEDIA

WILL HELP YOU, DO NOT PANIC, NEVER.
IT WILL HARK ON YOU TO GUIDE YOU.

Inspite of your mistakes you are a blessing. Lord comes to you in your vision. Vision as God is perfection in you. Do not look at your boss for salary, God is your sauce. Protection through vision, provision of God and your needs.

Deep reverential to Kaleakaye

Oh Kaleakaye Oh Kaleakaye Oh Kaleakaye,
You are the light and wisdom,
I love you I love you I love you,
I adore you I adore you I adore you.

Oh Kaleakaye Oh Kaleakaye Oh Kaleakaye
You are the good God and merciful,

To change us To change us To change us,
I adore you I adore you I adore you.

Oh Kaleakaye Oh Kaleakaye Oh Kaleakaye,
You are the respite God and forgiveful,
To deliver us To deliver us To deliver us,
I adore you I adore you I adore you.

Oh Kaleakaye Oh Kaleakaye Oh Kaleakaye,
You are the healing God and washeth our sins,
To give rebirth To give rebirth To give rebirth,
I adore you I adore you I adore you.

Oh Kaleakaye Oh Kaleakaye Oh Kaleakaye,
You are the answer and direction,
To give salvation To give salvation To give salvation,
I adore you I adore you I adore you.

Oh Kaleakaye Oh Kaleakaye Oh Kaleakaye,
You are the spirit of lord you are the spirit of lord you are
the spirit of lord,
To give liberty To give liberty To give liberty,
I adore you I adore you I adore you.

Oh Kaleakaye Oh Kaleakaye Oh Kaleakaye,
I listen your voice I listen your voice I listen your voice,
To give in one second the truth
I adore you I adore you I adore you.

Oh Kaleakaye Oh Kaleakaye Oh Kaleakaye,
You are the cosmos engulfing terrifying love,

To give simplicity a meaning To give simplicity a meaning
To give simplicity a meaning,
I adore you I adore you I adore you.

Oh Kaleakaye Oh Kaleakaye Oh Kaleakaye,
You are the God's desire,
To give kindled light,future, life beautiful To give kindled
light,future, life beautiful To give kindled light,future, life
beautiful,
I adore you I adore you I adore you.

Oh Kaleakaye Oh Kaleakaye Oh Kaleakaye,
The holy spirit moves,
It is unthinkeable to us,preach solutions,wisdom and God
It is unthinkeable to us,preach solutions,wisdom and God
It is unthinkeable to us,preach solutions,wisdom and God,
I adore you I adore you I adore you.

Oh Kaleakaye Oh Kaleakaye Oh Kaleakaye,
You are the eternal metaphysical time,
To cherish,be joyous and bath in elixir of life,
Let's bow down Let's bow down Let's bow down,
Lead us lead us lead us,
To fullness of dream of your heart,
To make us your sons and daughters to be a full life of
feetwashing unto you,

Oh Kaleakaye Oh Kaleakaye Oh Kaleakaye,
Let peace prevail Let peace prevail Let peace prevail.

Have and move mountains by faith. He will guide you continually and continued guidance you will receive. Faith is divine guidance.

By Faith By Faith By Faith By Faith.

These words should sink into your spirit, walking by faith is walking in divine guidance. Reach out and move out with divine guidance. Be guided in a divine manner. Meditate what the holy spirit has talked to you.

The 3 C's

COMMUNICATE

CHARITY (INVOLVED IN)

CALL TO PARTICIPATE IN GOD'S WORDS

Limbs be loosened, paralysis gone, open your heart to God, healing is yours, tell and have your soul talk with God. Walk! Walk! Walk! Walk! Walk! Walk! Walk! Walk! Walk!. We speak advancement in personal life, family, education and promotion. Our grandparent led the foundation of our trajectory,no matter what, do-not give up. We should know-more as "myself" initiative. Keep overcoming challenges, you are not alone overcome the difficulty,if others can overcome,you can also, situations can be overcome,gift of legacy is still of education,baby steps improvement leads to next goals. Freedom shall be so inspiring. Faith seed is passed from grandmother, mom to children and children's children. Faith in God can overcome any challenges. Legacy food assimilates to faith to trickle to compassion. If I can do it, I know you can do it. Pray your strategy for right start, faith and prayer. Fullness of dream of your heart bloom is in God. Rama-Buddha-Mohammed-Jesus is kind, holy and love. He is the revelation. Lord is looking for more than happy, healed people and real loyal friendship with Ramayana-Buddhist Texts-Quran-Bible. He establishes peace and loyalty and not "Democracy", as prince of joy, mercy and tenderness. Falling and loving for Rama-Buddha-Mohammed-Jesus is real dying,hardship, painstaking efforts and feet –washing, with clear message in mouth –teach all things that Rama-Buddha-Mohammed-Jesus commanded, that we are dying for salvation. Lord shows his glory, when oppression and slavery is pictured in democracy. Lord strikes the nation 10 times to bring water and food for son's and daughter's. God moves in unprecedented power to show his glory, essence and testimony as provider, with mighty hands and power dimension at core of your heart,whirl-wind of nuclear power that is prevailing like a protective layer between God and us. Rama-Buddha-Mohammed-Jesus will liberate you to commend attention to redefine holiness meaning. The pain of being lost of Rama-Buddha-Mohammed-Jesus is not seeing the trees of paradise, he could be mine for ever and I for him for ever, for what we are dying for,show us the RAMA-BUDDHA-MOHAMMED-JESUS. Get their one second glimpse and ready to die, because that is liberty, holding as a mirage, the glory of the Lord,from glory to glory there is liberty. Crisis of nation with Gospel beauty, bring glory with fire and authority, light will overcome darker, it rose again to be lit up as

World. Receive mercy, do not lose heart. We should love each other. You become what you behold,the selfishness of Rama-Buddha-Mohammed-Jesus. Let there be power and light bloom by holy-spirit. Do not preach for selves but preach within. Best basketball player Michael Jordan plays basketball-preach within. Holy spirit is God's GPS, turn around and make a U-turn, to head towards home direction, by making a shift. Great revival is great turning towards God, may be micro or at country level. Stealing became less, crime seized, jails vacated, saved animals, air of compassion prevailed, people gave back money they owed, GDP of country increased, growth rate increased. God is going to save 10,00,000 people and more around the world,in dramatic move of God, as revival tendency. All grey area of our lives may be removed changed peoples direction to positive. Time does not take care of sin,carrying sin is dying according to scriptures, please repent and move towards Rama-Buddha-Mohammed-Jesus.We cannot hide our sin. Adam and Eve after sinning wrapped –hided by God from fig leaves to animal skin, killing animal is a sin,Rama-Buddha-Mohammed-Jesus took the pain and burden,their blood and sweat hided you from sin.

33 QUESTIONS TOWARD GOD'S PATH AND REINFORCEMENT THAT, GOD IS ALSO BEING WITH YOU.

1. DO YOU PRAY TO GOD?
2. DO YOU VISUALISE GOD IN MEAL TIME?
3. DO YOU PRAY IN OTHERS SUCCESS?

4. DO YOU TEND TOWARDS GOD?
5. DO YOU REMAIN ALOOF FROM ACCOMPLISHMENT CREDIT?
6. DO YOU VISUALISE GOD IN SLEEPING TIME?
7. DO YOU VISUALISE GOD IN ALL DAILY CHORES?
8. YOU ADMIT YOUR SUCCESS IS BY GOD.
9. YOU DO NOT MURMUR OR GRIEVE AGAINST GODS WILL AND BE WITH GOD.
10. YOU TREAT ALL EQUALLY.
11. YOU LOVE NEIGHBOURS.
12. AT OFFICE PEERS ARE BROTHERS, AND SISTERS.
13. YOU SING THE LORD'S WORDS.
14. YOU TRY TO PLACE TO PRAY DAILY.
15. YOU DO NOT THINK BAD ABOUT OTHERS.
16. YOU DO NOT BAD-MOUTH OTHERS.
17. YOU VALUE MARRIAGE AND UNIVERSAL BONDING.
18. YOU VALUE ALL GENDER TO BE GOD'S CREATION.
19. YOU ARE CHILDLIKE INNOCENT.
20. YOU PRAY FOR POSITIVE SUCCESS OF OTHERS.
21. IN YOU, EVIL CANNOT STAY AND HIDE AS A DUNGEON.
22. GOD'S WILL AND GOD'S ETHER WILL PREVAIL IN YOU.
23. YOU THINK, SMELL, VISUALISE, HEAR, SPEAK, TOUCH, TOWARDS GOD, IN

PHYSICALLY AND PARTICIPATE IN GOD'S WORDS ETHEREALLY.

24. YOUR NEW YEAR RESOLUTION IS TENDING TOWARDS GOD.
25. YOU REMAIN ALOOF FROM MAL AIR.
26. YOU REMAIN ALOOF FROM DRUGS AND MEDICINES AS GOD HAS CHOSEN YOU.
27. YOU REMAIN ALOOF FROM ADDICTIVE DRUGS AND PORNOGRAPHY.
28. YOUR THEME OF DEVELOPMENT IS MICRO AND MACRO AND NOT AGAINST DEMOCRACY.
29. YOU ARE SOLUTION ORIENTED AND COLLECTIVE.
30. YOU ARE GODLY AND RAMA-BUDDHA-MOHAMMED-JESUS LIKE.
31. YOU ARE FAMILY ORIENTED, TEND CHILDREN AND COOK FOOD FOR WIFE.
32. YOU NATURALLY LOVE AND NURTURE CHILDREN.
33. YOU HAVE A THIRST FOR OTHER CITIZENRY.

God has plans for future and something more for you. God answers the desires of our heart sometimes, always and sometimes not.

God lives in our nations. You must trust lord in all our heart. You should really-really believe that you are child of God and you dwell in God's country. I found something to live for and found something to die for.

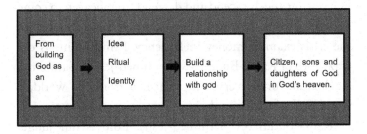

A stronger ties of past, present, future with beyond planes relationship with God. God change my circumstances,even if you don't I will have stronger ties and faith unto you. After the snake the Adam and Eve sinned, satan came,and holes are the mark of satanic serpent in our body and atmosphere. On the final D Day, satan will be on opposite side, backed by satanic order, God will be on opposite side backing you,as your defender, the final verdict will be put toward you to protect you from death circles and give another life-blessed. Satan will directly and indirectly take you towards vows of death,and will complain on your sins list as checkmated by God to you,you will tremble,Gods will pray for you,God will show you his power and real workings unto you,you shall surrender and lead in prayer so that you need him and he will fill your D Day and D life,first remain aloof from pornography, adultery, bad habits, sexual exploitation trafficking…,you do have transformed and beaten the devil by God's challenge to enter his bosom of faith,remain as another life-blessed. Do not chase prophecy,chase God's heart to dive into God's faith.

PUT YOUR FAITH INTO ACTION

Physical miracles unto you in God's plane unto your plane. Harvesting angels ascend and descend from heaven to come and be present in your circumstance to take you out of the crisis example money inefficiency. Family,home is the crazy love of Rama-Buddha-Mohammed-Jesus. Gambling, alcohol, stealing, everything vanished from the world, a world full of peace and simplicity, is the guarantee seal of Rama-Buddha-Mohammed-Jesus. Lord is our judge, law giver, and king to solve our problems. He will decide our winning and losing. It is the descending voice of righteousness you will have. When you stand you will get promoted. By standing, you are raised upto another level for promotion, he will manifest inside. Prayer can turn around any situation of your life. When righteousness is in authority people rejoice. The wicked perturbs people and causes problems. Lord touches wickedness for people to rejoice. Corrupting, like bribes damages the spirit of country. Some of the richest places with rich resources, have 3 phase growing seasons to have full bloom. We need to be brutally honest unlike flattery and being hypocrite. Wages of enjoyment with sin is death. Result of sin is anger, greed, selfishness, bitterness in heart, and so on,unending list. Serve God and poor rather serving wicked and sin. A wise man walking in humility,turns away from wrath, a city is saved, moral vs vile, light vs dark, God vs sin, righteousness vs conviction, a wise man reasons God and needs him,keeps his mouth shut,as all the servants are wicked. If you have faith in God, you cannot be in dungeon, of direct and indirect purposely sinning, as God resides –lives inside you.

WE MUST HAVE REVERENTIAL FEAR THAT GOD IS WATCHING ALL THE TIME.

WE MUST HAVE REVERENTIAL FEAR THAT GOD IS WATCHING ALL THE TIME.

I LOVE PEOPLE TO INVEST NOW, FOR LATER ON. THERE ARE PEOPLE WHO DO THE WRONG THING, GAMBLERS THAT THINK THEY ARE DOING WELL, BUT IN GOD'S WILL FABRIC AND WORDS PAY-OFF WILL DECLINE.

EDUCATION IS THE KNOWLEDGE WE HAVE AND WISDOM IS BEYOND US.

DO NOT DO IT, IT IS NOT PEACE, THY MIND WEIGHS PROS AND CONS ,KNOWLEDGE COMES LATER, WISDOM IS THE INWARD PARTS, INWARD PARTS ARE QUICKER THAN BRAIN ,NOW GOD HAS PREVAILED .YOU GIVE ME THE VERSES IN HEART.

SPENDING TIME WITH GODS FABRIC, WORDS IS HOUSE TO ALL FLESH, IT IS MEDICINE FOR CRITICAL DISEASES LIKE CANCER, MANY ARE RESPONDING TO GOSPEL. BUT EVIL MEN WILL GROW WORSE AND WORSE IF WE DO NOT GIVE THEM DEFINITION OF LIFE. GOD AND RAMA-BUDDHA-MOHAMMED-JESUS IS FRIEND TO SINNER, CASTED OUT DEMONS, HEALING, LIFTING, ENCOURAGING AND DRIVING ALWAYS –ALWAYS-ALWAYS. THEY HAD NO INEQUITY TOWARDS SINNERS

MOVE FROM HOPE(GOD IN YOU) TO FAITH (JOYFUL CONFIDENT EXPECTATION WHAT GOD WILL DO FOR YOU),DO NOT CONFORM TO STANDARDS, MOVE IN GLORY AND PERFECTION ,INHERITANCE OF GOD ,PROBLEMS ARE PART OF LIFE ,BUT GOD HAS GIVEN US THIS NEW SYSTEM TO CONQUER ,BY WORD AND RENEWING OUR MIND-MEDITATING IN THE WILL AND OF LORD ,AND THEN YOU WILL HAVE A NEW WALK.

There is nothing better than knowing you did the right thing. The by-product of righteousness is your doing. So never worry, get involved in it, obey Lord, and you did the right thing. Be not worry in doing the right thing. Do not worry if you are waiting long time for doing the right thing. I will obey God that little things he tells me to do. Everything you tried to do, everything came from self. God is righteous in making sinner righteous. Commitment, daily confession about word of God, is the honey lemon crush. Daily devotion principles repeated again and again, power of spoken word, let there be set,not only the ability to reason but to repeat confession word, to speak creatively. When you are in Lord, Lord protects you. Lord comes for your defence, even if he hires a judge. Dark hates the life, abomination to unjust-wicked. Evil, darkness hates light. It is not the symbolic name of wisdom, or, but no knowledge of wisdom, it is the word and light of God. God is the universal supreme, engulfer of the world, the almighty powerful. It's doing what is right, particularly feeling not doing right,is not important if we do what God asks us to do in our life,then we will emerge victorious. I am not dictated by what flesh tells to do but by the spirit to do the holy feet-washing. We will reap what we sow. Self-control is an amazing freedom, no cookies and pastry can disturb you. God doesn't give self-control, so that we can control anybody other's lives, but self-lives. Sometimes the answer doesn't come the same day but next day, but answer will come, the prince will declare your victory. The real iron-man is humbles by soft voice that breaks the bone. A soft tongue is so powerful. Hero's are tough. Devil uses music to trap and corrupt the youth, but has no wisdom. Because wisdom comes from Lord and cannot emanate from devil. We limbically search for Sati, Kaleakaye, Almaie and offer prayer in obeisance to the Lord, the Earth, Water, Air, Fire, Sky, Ether,Wood, Time, Wisdom, Hope, Patience, Healing, Love, Work. Miracle working powerfully, but devil blurs the recognition of miracle, mind it. Keeping rules so that you are righteous under God's sight, Under law but under grace,they turn into gifts. Your sins cannot condemn you. This boy was born to save. Lord is always with you to always prosper you.

REAL BATTLE IS IN HEAVEN, THE THINGS THAT ARE UNSEEN IS ETERNAL AND TRUTH, UNLIKE THINGS SEEN.

3

D GATEWAY-OMNIPRESENCE

If Rama-Buddha-Mohammed-Jesus as a person Lord did not exist in name and identity then such other person did exist in any other name and identity with supreme personality of Godhead and an apotheosis of God and human perfection or else a collective entity was driving the India and world family as names of Rama-Buddha-Mohammed-Jesus as persons Lords existing in name and identity as the only personal saviour the supreme Godhead in the same bucket of water if it was truth as in Blavatskian Theosophy.If such persons could be an integration in lives regulating the earth family today from the times of formation of universe,leading an exemplary collective droplets from the same grand universal tankers. Then if we unify these droplets to a single tricklet derivative then Rama-Buddha-Mohammed-Jesus as a person God with name and identity with universal supreme Godhead was born,transformed and lived amongst us. Food, healing, miracles; Rama-Buddha-Mohammed-Jesus casted many demons out to make them nobler; Rama-Buddha-Mohammed-Jesus casted many demons out to heal them and reveal the lords divinity and eternal truth ; Rama-Buddha-Mohammed-Jesus touched the lives, their personal touch brought everlasting changes and strengthened universal brethrenity; their exemplary leadership transformed human minds and atoms, flora and fauna for the truth to prevail, and universal codes to prevail, unify strengthen and prevail glorify. In Rama-Buddha-Mohammed-Jesus leadership limbic system leadership / contingency leadership / chinnamastaka's mindset / grey area leadership / transformational leadership is marked. If Rama-Buddha-Mohammed-Jesus did not exist why history as a personality was so strong in voicing, airing, spreading, benchmarking, reinforcing,transforming and creating entities from nanoscule to tera-level and infinitesimal,reflecting in personal lives of civilians the happiness and joy of receiving Lord Rama-Buddha-Mohammed-Jesus; the transcendental development of technology from primitive to International conglomerate,of Space Station Era,where the triune Godheads merge to seek,establish the chinnamastaka's leadership, re-reading the Rama-Buddha-Mohammed-Jesus truth and bringing a truthful democracy co-ordinates of a simple, developing, self-correcting society where we the world family get eternal bliss, divinity, and quantum leap in material control; ultimately merging with supreme Godhead. Image and mental space description of Rama-Buddha-Mohammed-Jesus, cannot be soulfully written and captured in canvas but co-ordinates can be mapped to some extent. The praise of Lord, word of Lord, name of Lord is the body of Lord and soul of Lord. Lord shall bless the soul and Lord shall pour all his benefits on you. Who forgives all your iniquities and heals all your diseases. Who redeems your life from pit of corruption. He satisfies your mouth with God and renews your youth like eagle.

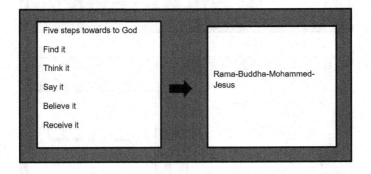

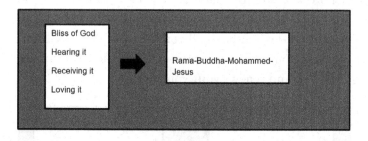

Bliss of God

Hearing it

Receiving it

Loving it

→ Rama-Buddha-Mohammed-Jesus

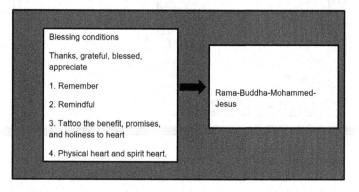

Blessing conditions

Thanks, grateful, blessed, appreciate

1. Remember

2. Remindful

3. Tattoo the benefit, promises, and holiness to heart

4. Physical heart and spirit heart.

→ Rama-Buddha-Mohammed-Jesus

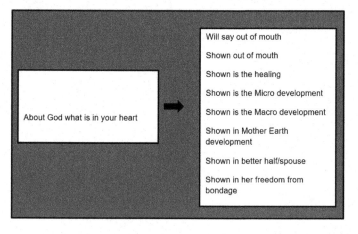

About God what is in your heart

→

Will say out of mouth

Shown out of mouth

Shown is the healing

Shown is the Micro development

Shown is the Macro development

Shown in Mother Earth development

Shown in better half/spouse

Shown in her freedom from bondage

You cannot connect to your future until you disconnect from past. Pain and peace cannot be at the same time. Two season warring with one another. Our natural seasons chained. You cannot help two seasons at same time. If the old does not go new cannot come.

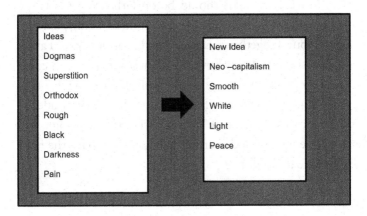

Ultimately we fall in love with pain and peace sons.

Stages of DISCONNECT

1. LETTING GO
2. DECLARING AN END
3. NEW PURSUIT

Ultimately we fall in permanent connection.

Father Jesus, Prophet, Sai, Krishna, Parsuram, Rama, Jagannath, Mahatma, Nelson, Peter Drucker, Teresa, Pope Francis, Pope John Paul II, Vivekananda, Ramakrushna Paramhamsa, Gurunanak, Gautam Buddha, John, Jacob, Exodus, Hazrat Ali, Moses, Elizah, Jehovah, Joseph, Mary,

Fatima, Sita, Hanuman, Laxman,determines the mirror of our relationship with Father and God, his relationship with Father and God, God's relationship with Father and God. "I" am the way, the truth and white, destination was the father. Jesus told Father is greater than him. Father who is in heaven,our focus should be on father,so Jesus is the Father,and through the Father. The Father's loving plan that all are bound together. A strong bond relationship of Father God, no God is daddy but through Jesus, no one can come to Father God but through Jesus. Father is first in Christian walk. You know how much Father loves you-Rama-Buddha-Mohammed-Jesus. There is no situation that can come and postpone it, it is God that maketh it. People have the faith to believe it,make it.

Crumbs in! Crumbs in! Crumbs in! Crumbs in! Crumbs in! Crumbs in! Crumbs in!

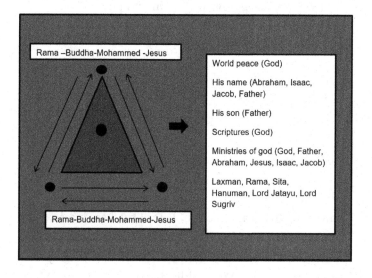

God is to visit that again and pull it out because you are not so ordinary in evangelical Jesus, Rama, Sai, Krishna, Prophet, Parsuram, Jagannath and Gautam Buddha. The damsel is not dead but it is sleeping merrily and you are unbelief that you cannot sleep. The Lord listens always, they are out there in a big promotion. There was an immediate situation, situation, emergency, pressing, demanding wrong scapel, to pull out, outside in yard still happy, Jesus heard the servant, always do obvious, from birth to death, honour the servant. Remember felling, prayer words coming and disappearing, other people praying too, hope was lost, browsing to the poem, I am not doing my way but through others way, the glory of you not established but the Father, Abba's glory established. To bring the inner bound body, gross cries that Shalom, God bless you, what I said,is the answer,the home, think about, astray all my son, my entities, people use you to fall to baptise but the Guru is one, because our Abba slept, everything is my goodness, I lost you, because life came from my body, he said voice is my ministry, my sorrow is a miracle, the only one that needs no miracles are those that saw it and are never given. You find in scriptures, seen most sorrows, concerned all, thou to also, that is riding tomb in bible, unreed touched, Jesus ok, resurrected, rebuke me, power yourself, in doubt, God is travelling your lines with GPS 231,outskirts,it tries to criss-cross you at GPS 431,UnGPS and true doubt, i.e is called true now, then true believe, then true help, then true getting, then get to know, then pastor everywhere neo body to sue every bodieth that search God shalt findeth me and watched TOM, whole time made to bow my sin, (ALLAH-YOU).He did it for you. Time was going,belief had sued faith, if faction was, untime it,it was not the same condition of the child. The universe and friends were going because faith was at top, the Bible said God was at top, Jesus was rewarded, tolerated flesh, faced everything in life, untidied life, say like Job- I persuade cheap, let devil tell your faith.. the word FEAR, and Lo! Behold Chinnamastaka shall appear, to nourish it with nectar. Nectar is Chinnamastaka- Fear is God. Then fear to say God! God! God! God! God! God!. Rest in peace, knowledge, God, Super the Supernatural. Then say Supernatural! Supernatural! Supernatural! Supernatural! Supernatural! Supernatural! Supernatural!.

Father says come to Allah, Allah says come to Father it is not Father but Profoundness that is the matter. RAMA-BUDDHA-MOHAMMED-JESUS gets uncomfortable close to you to meet your salvation. Enzyme substrate cataclysyms work well in this model to achieve higher nascent or bonded synergistic states. By steaming we clear the food,from sins.

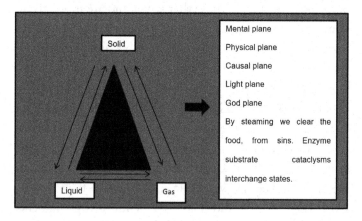

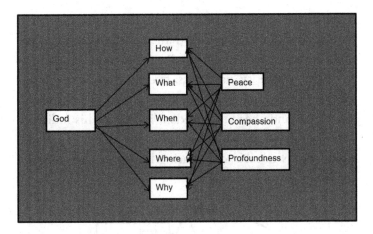

Sin, degradation, disease is breaking and stopping our plane and God's plane and enter of entity in status quo state.

Healing and freedom

Walking the sun way ; Vit-D

Clouds rain (Weep)-a Matrika; the lightening roar (a roar of Matrika to present at times of your difficulties and delivering you from bondage)the thunder,(the roar voice of Matrika to be present at times of your difficulties and deliver you from bondage),smell actinomycetes suddenly and balance serenely.

The plants and animals and micro-organisms (flora and fauna healing and subtle dynamicity); the Hanuman / Matrika/ Kaleakaye / Chamundaye to deliver Rama from bondage. They do Talk with you and understand your emotions and deliver you.

You can feel in your aura, spirit, soul the effervescence but not the physical heat,the warmth,the healing rays and fusion and fission to Vit D,healing and synthesis with abundancy in wealth,prosperity, happiness, freedom, joy, eternal bliss, eternal feetwashing, as freedom is the quantum threshold status quo and ahead,the freedom is yours. This indicates Matrikas presence,your emotions as joy circles of human flower beads to take to,to roaring leaps and new freedom levels but also abundancy.

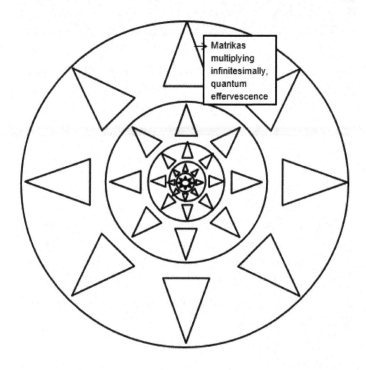

Matrikas multiplying infinitesimally, quantum effervescence

The earth revolves, takes you in its Lap as Matrikas feeds you its milk and shows cuddled freedom,a birth right and only your Mama. It shall cuddle you,wave at you and lap you.

The water you bathe, drink, splash, sprinkle nourishes, allows you to cuddly and bubbly grow and make you energetic and healing angels with washing of sins and taking of sins by boiling from its entities, the more you boil meat with water, sin is taken, it tastes good, and edible and healthy. The water has undergone the entity of Rama and Matrika, it shall welcome you, deliver you and free you from bondage as the Rama and Matrika, Father's way of lag, growth, log and abundancy, a status quo of always, sins of abundancy of "Bhandar Griha", the Bhandar Kaleakaye Matrika leads.

Air we breathe, the quantum breeze we subtly feel is the Matrika, with its wind power and gusts moves the Coconut and Casuarina and the bridges and roars the lions way that "I" am present. Its healing Matrikas help to change the solar system and move in sync with laws of karma-the quantum "me" and "Matrika"-the feeder and restorer of universal freedom and healthy healing and prosperity. It shall welcome you with serenity. Fire roars, proclaims victory as well seeks you, chaste you, virgin you, purify you, to walk in union with solar system to hasten and fasten your belief that its consent is your spiritual quotient. Working for the Solar Matrika as an entity Matrika with Karma of "me" and "Matrika" –more oxygen, good medium, good combustible vapours, good energy, good purification, good repentance, a lead of sin-free life –philanthropy, gospel speech, and uplifting the poor, the bondage is ending because status quo is freedom. Fire radiance, glow, luminosity, welcome with warmth. Sky is in golden throne and and disguise room, where entities pervade and Matrikas multiply. The heaven cherishingly meet and hell gets away, correctify Earth

Matrika and entity sleeps, dwells, and bubbles sin free. "Me" and "Matrika" relationship is strengthened by hug, race and milk-food. Sky is the realm of joy, the goodness of sky blue and ether. Ether the Matrika ruler that sets all Matrikas free. Where quantum starts and ends and sets you free. The ethereal violet is in Aha !-effect. Wood, the Lord Jagannath rules the kingdom in Bagala Wand and Dasavatar "change manifestations" leading to a freedom. Wood is the splendour and grandeur in its being and aura and it is auspicious. Time–is faith the fusion –fission circular Matrikas of all logs to intimate "I am there". Time is the eternal you. Wisdom is the Saraswati Lord. Hope is your entity. Patience is your entity. Receiving Healing is your birth entity. Love is your milk-feed from entity. Work the Jesus way of feet-washing and sans bondage, stalwart moving in Matrikas lines,as Matrika is in sole motive, mover as dance of twigs and branches with air bearing fruits for sparrows. In Rama's period as Rama waged and solved problems of rural brethren and rural communities,abundance and granary problems, exchange problems with rural input suppliers and sahukars,ancient ingot, exchangers and cowries for lending money to do a deal barter/closure and exchange for food ;Rama dealt with it. Alienic presence brought enlightenment in Rama's lives, supernatural ingenuity of supreme universal comfort and soothe his problems, to every of his mobilization strangest ardous, blue-moon, unthought, never-before-heard and listened, compelling vulnerable,near –death experience problems there is a light but infinitesimal comfort, healing, soothing and compassionating and soul consoling subtle Miracle from the solar galaxial heavenly soul-realms to bring supernatural saviour armour a seat –bed on the God's womb and lap and divine nectar to suckle from your birth right. Lord Vishnu and aliens come on earth to wield the Bridge-Setu for reaching Lankeswar Kingdom over Indian Ocean with courage, technology- archetype; state-of -art never before boasted and achieved,risk –taking,problem solving,leadership of Lord Sugriva, Lord Jambavan, Hanuman and Lord Squirrel with Hanuman's, firmly confidence instilling,joy shouts,and try again actions in minds of Sugriv Sena, a transformational

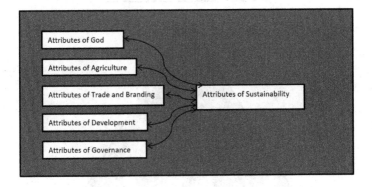

Sustainability/ Ecosystem Balance Matrix Model

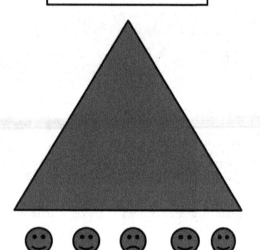

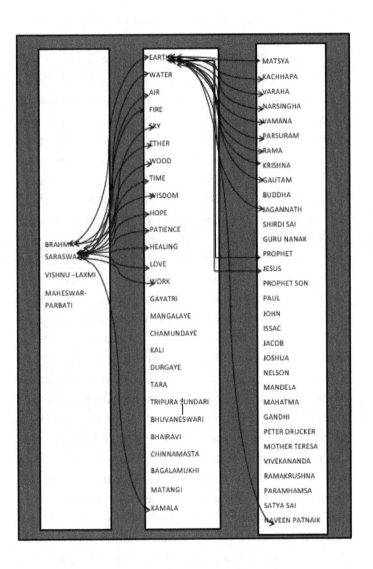

Above Sustainability dynamicity model

leadership for Rama in overall to reach-touch Sita Maa.The entire Ayodhya was happy by the change. Please trust God and do good. Rama-Sita eras, aeons shows elixir of life. Lord Earth, Water, Air, Fire, Sky, Ether, Wood commingles with the energy Lord, harvested Goldmines and alienic intervention helped in glory of the administration and supernatural abundance in forest, rural vicinities.The time horizon bowed for its feetwashing, of the Lord as Supreme Cosmos Universal Energy Lord God Vishnu himself. Regressing of the Lords or Rama-Sita brought sin-washing and abundance. Eras and aeons of regressings brought infinitesimal peace, divine bliss, happiness, eternality in time, and divine heavenly abode on earthly abode. God is the good God, pardoning God, delivering God, healing God, thy washeth your sins, thy solves your problems, thy is with you, always the one that solves your problem, supports you, suckles you, takes your hards yokes and doeseth for you to prevail eternal peace, eternal bliss, heavenly abode earthly realms, eternal affection and choral angelic hands to heal and help. The energy Aha! Burst-walking with God by his hands holding you,and he always around you, with his contagious compassion and smile. The energy sum total moves in sync with other energies and entities giving an Aha-burst, effect as temporal in time machine and in matter as spatial,both dimential degrees, infinitesimal as with energy of Earth, Water, Air,Fire, Sky, Ether, Wood, Time, Wisdom, Hope, Patience, Healing, Love, Work. They commingle, heal, destinize, benchmark, search for excellence and merge with excellence. Either as entity with entity, entity on other entity or regressing of entity on other or correlation of one with other or structurating an equation model in lines of distributive justice of entity at sans Maya, you are competing against yourself and not against others,breathing freely, quietness, effervescence, brain storming bubbliness, joyfulness, oneness, compassion that is infectious and contagious, cohesion molecules of development, giving rise to joy-joy rides,atomic thresholds trans-spins, referential and time-bound Karmic ups and downs roller coaster,the kink and again within circles and you-you oneness rides.

Visualising God

God through visions, insights and dreams, talks to you, you can feel God through such entities. I have seen God. Angels do talk to me and give me profound and vivid visions, insights and dreams. God is the supernatural entity in your life to bring supernatural abundance, happiness, joy, smile, eternal help, blissful healing. Cohesive molecules unite, commingle for win-win situation, Gods vision insights and dreams are infectious win-win situations in your life, aura of joyous-joyous circles, energy abundance of entities,and show abundance in wealth, health, insights, help and co-operation, co-opetition, relationship,ethics, familyship, communityship and blissful workship, are harbinger of an entities which on regressed brings other entities to bubble up and work with united hands to again win-win circles.

Universal Mother

She is the universal Mama, fondly and cheerful. She takes you in her lap, she is the good Mama, always thinking about you and caressing you, in her lap, fondling you with her nectar, washing away your sins and making you a good personality. She is with you. She is besides your times at distress at toughness times. She holds you to time and puts entities as you grow, nurture with the time commingle, as entity time paves your win-win strides. The degrees of time suiting you pave for bliss of the Lord. The supreme universal mother embarks on a journey through you, with her entities and past co-ordinate regressants emerging win-win and(co-operation + competition) co-opetition,with innovation and simplicity. The ultimate path is the doorway of sacred,pure, whiteness, eternal, nectary bliss as the Lord appear,so in your life victory appears leading to immense,belief that Lord is the true friend,mother, guide, voice, and steadship. In agonies and pain,mother rises, aliens rise, angels rise, heavenly realms rise, galaxial waves rise, quantum transmutation, spintronics, spin-offs, vibrations co-opetition and cohese and sync, commingle,compassion molecules, mother, shows tranformationist humbleness in weaving goal, vision, work queue, to lead as epitome for founding preliminary savioural lines for your present times by prodigally working your DNA,conflict–DNA, and Godly DNA, for win-win-path. Win-win is now,this moment, today, this time, this hour, this minute, this second as your respite with time sense-mother in lap-cuddle to take you in her embodiment the Supreme infinitesimal beingful mother; again bliss,so why do you repent, your mother,us at your bedside, workplace, painstakes situation and bondage.

DNA Freedom

Vasuki and Kaliye hypnotise you from time to time. We remain in self-deception. Self-deception is a natural defence from bad fat and bad destiny. Molecular entities cohese and vibrate and keep you in self-deception mode, the by default, it is goodness made from bad fat to keep your DNA guarded from oxidiser, as anti-oxidants surround DNA to keep them in natural freedom and nascent activity stage for expression multitudeness. On your development journey realms keeping finally, your DNA, again in effervescent freedom, and expression. Vasuki and Kaliye guarded ShreeKrishna, a serpent always was seen in Shaivite's upper position of Universal supreme merge-head. Its speed is light and sword and mental realms experience. Swift movement of positive thought as those around them. Words hypnotise us and sting us to give sarcasm and humblity to tolerance nand submissiveness and bow-head nodding down as down to earth humbleness. It takes you on a surge ahead towards universal supreme distributor of eternal life-head and pure white mama and daddy.

Friendship and Relationship

A good company is worth "priceless". A person only seeking the Lord has lord's friendship and relationship within him. Use of coercion, bad language, plots, and secret missions to achieve work is the bondage of entity. Entity is infinitesimal. The sum total of energy in this universe is constant. It pervades Earth, Water, Air, Fire, Sky, Ether, Wood, Time,

Wisdom, Hope, Patience, Healing, Love And Work. One cannot use such things always as structurating in cohese model of entities as well as regressants on each other with strength and degree,correlation shows an upsurge of aura rise of iquity towards the vulnerable,as it is seen,when in a Nobel Laurette show God reigns and positive prevail,so also with needy and meek the surge is,seen to hiddenly help him/her in the struggle with victory of Lords name in angelic surrounds of heavenly realms of Godhead. To every action there is equal and opposite reaction, the person uttered the person as is, and the person reapeth as is, so God shows the right –the right and the referential right God shows, the referential right, the point of view, right entity shows point of view right, the with respect to right God shows,with respect to right, with perspective right God shows perspective right, to relative term right, God shows relative term of right. Why does God take away the favourite toy from the child, so that you focus on almighty and have spiritual maturity. You are branded,sealed and maketh by Holy spirit.

Life, family, relationship is a function of			
Earth	Chinna-mastaka's presence- faith	Ethereal water cleansing dirt towards faith belief: you are his and she is yours, born for each other.	Supernatural faith belief.
Water	Chinna-mastaka's presence- fire	Love bath: you are his and she is yours, born for each other, eternal birth for each other.	Supernatural purity; innate oneness, divine love –bath, beingfullness, effulgence.
Air	Chinna-mastaka's presence-work		
Fire	Chinna-mastaka's presence- bow	Feet washing: you are his and she is yours, born for each other.	Supernatural devotion.
Sky		Godly light union: I can do all things because God is my strength, we both can do all things because God is my/our strength.	Supernatural union with supreme God-head
Ether	Chinna-mastaka's presence-sound		
Wood			
Time	Chinna-mastaka's presence-worship	Melodious God Fidel sound-bells and drums: desire and passion to do for god by understanding you through your voice sounds to lub-dub heart rhythms.	Supernatural voice.
Wisdom			
Hope	Chinna-mastaka's presence-brand	Daily beginning of God's praise chant.	Supernatural worship.
Patience			
Healing		Fidel brand: God has sealed you with everlasting relationship.	Supernatural Fidel brand-image personality.
Love	Chinna-mastaka's presence-initiation		
Work		Supernatural thirst passion.	Supernatural cradle bath beginnings.

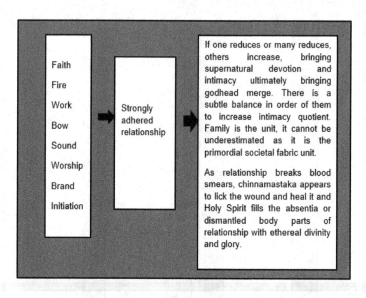

Faith
Fire
Work
Bow
Sound
Worship
Brand
Initiation

→

Strongly adhered relationship

→

If one reduces or many reduces, others increase, bringing supernatural devotion and intimacy ultimately bringing godhead merge. There is a subtle balance in order of them to increase intimacy quotient. Family is the unit, it cannot be underestimated as it is the primordial societal fabric unit.

As relationship breaks blood smears, chinnamastaka appears to lick the wound and heal it and Holy Spirit fills the absentia or dismantled body parts of relationship with ethereal divinity and glory.

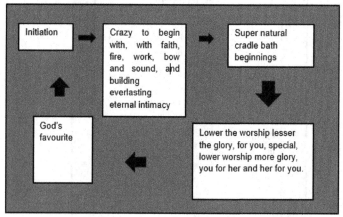

Initiation

→

Crazy to begin with, with faith, fire, work, bow and sound, and building everlasting eternal intimacy

→

Super natural cradle bath beginnings

God's favourite

Lower the worship lesser the glory, for you, special, lower worship more glory, you for her and her for you.

LORD FEEDETH THE TINY SPARROWS, YOU ARE WORTH MORE.

4

SACROSANCT GLORY

Foods in birth of Rama and Laxman taken by queen (payasam);mention in Ganesha and Shiva scriptural texts,existence of Ladoos for offering to Lord Ganesha the welcome and auspicious and eternal form of entity at lords feets before worship and grants of ageless wishes from the destroyer of evil and dawn of all entities in the cosmos the Lord God Ganesha and showerer of ethereal realms and peace keeper.From this logic we can conclude the practice of pulses and oilseeds and their abundance since the inception era of formation and growth of civilization with rich realms of supreme God centroids of Matsya, Kurma, Varaha, Nrusingha, Vamana, Parsuram, Rama, Krishna, Buddha, Kalki incarnations.There is existence of paddy mentioned in Ramcharitmanas consumed by queens in form of payasam for giving birth to Rama and laxman. The most auspicious offering to Lord till date on earth in this Godly times is paddy.Paddy offerings has been widely accepted to all Gods in all regional cultures and global cultures in India,Africa,China,Japan,Middle –East,and some parts of Northern Hemispheres.Paddy since time immemorial formed the infinitesimal cosmos for feeding the growing nascent civilizations and had the aura of healing it. The recent works of scientists of NRRI erstwhile CRRI Odisha,of incorporating the anti-diabetic gene in Lalat Paddy var.shows powerful and subtle dynamicity of linkages of baton of auspicious paddy's trajectory since times of inception till the Jagannath culture of Odisha as well also linking with Beta-carotene enriched rice by Ingo Potrykos.This shows the Godly Aura of paddy in eradication of poverty and global malnutrition with its humbleness in historical march of civilization and a continuity baton of steadfastness establishing a clear path of chinnamastaka's desire for ultimate ether to its cradle-bath children proving her existence since the Matsya, Kurma, Varaha, Nrusingha, Vamana, Parsuram, Rama, Krishna, Buddha, Kalki incarnations,clearly paving as Yuga Sahasra, commingling with time and space,light and sound,proactively thinking the future times of limbic contingency and supernatural cradle-bath existence of children. Farming practices were unique in inception times as well as in Rama, Buddha, Mohammed and Jesus period. The modern engineered practices of line transplanting and line sowing were ultra-modernly and dedicatedly practiced in Rama, Buddha, Mohammed and Jesus period. Civilians had deep understanding of agriculture more sophisticated than modern agriculture with dynamicity of supernatural dimensions in cultivars, time and space expansion of agriculture and systems and holistics in agriculture. The modern day gene technology and B.T. variants and genetically engineered variants are nothing but nanoscule degrees in findings from super-nature cultivated variants of paddy,pulses and oilseeds. The development of channel irrigation with monitored nutrient management as super-nature controlled with outlook of scarce resource management,depletion dynamics study and equity theory boomed the civilians with a rich and power soil with ultra-modern gully and sheet erosion and ravine erosion management and soil –life management with an auspicious crop husbandry. The water harvesting structures were prominent, engineered and state of art. Application of organic entities, was a philosophy and go of life which led to gamut of a crop-husbandry. Agronomic practices were beyond human intelligentia, intervention of Aliens for engineered technology led to a balanced exchequer, in Rama, Buddha,Mohammad, and Jesus period. Mother's presence in this ageold kitchen shows,her selfishness towards the cradle –bath of children feeding millions with divine nectar milk,with profound uniqueness,but equity centroiding,around the common arc of humanity,the true compassion mirror of Mother revealed in her cradle-bath of children,all limbic-leadership shall be yours vis-à-vis your unique children whose conscience and peace-keeping is your true heart revelation equating with Rama-Buddha-Mohammed-Jesus, the circle of lotus and roses of this cosmos family, but for you a petal and last but not the least to the savant, a crumb of petal again mark my words, Mother has appeared with equity, equanimity, freedom, ahimsa, eternal truth also marking Gandhian leadership of non-violence; again Mother dismantling non-existing entity with touch–battle, conceiving in her womb,giving the life blood and making a cradle-bath womb, infinitesimal processes repeated, a Rama, Buddha, Mohammed, Jesus, Krishna, Gandhi, Mother Teresa, Peter Drucker, Nelson Mandela is born ;but lo! again a cradle-bath touch ;like the quantum tuning fork dancing,quantum vibration of molecules, molecules displacing from mean position and gathering threshold positions and jumping to upper,similar and optimised threshold positions; and go-cart repetition: a Rama, Buddha, Mohammed, Jesus, Krishna, Gandhi, Mother Teresa, Peter Drucker, Nelson Mandela is again born. Doesn't Mother appear to us again and again, mark my words, goes the nectar milk with which goes are equity. In between cosmic vibrations,beatings to me, the logic is simple,humble, clear, meaningful, efficient and effective that if Mother is appearing before us in Time, Space, Light, Sound, Earth, Water, Air, Fire, Sky, Ether, Wood, Wisdom, Hope, Patience, Healing, Love,Work so also the ever humble,bowing banyan tree,its nectary milk with God's divine eternal equity,equanimity, freedom, ahimsa, non-violence eternal truth. The beatings tide again Mother appears to give eternal hope,nectary milk of equity. This marks the "THE END OF POVERTY AND IMMORTAL BRAND EQUITY SOUL CODES". Leadership preservation, creation, and innovation of Subash Chandra Bose, Mahatma Gandhi, Naveen Patnaik, Mother Teresa, Nelson Mandela, Peter Drucker, and eras leadership preservation, creation and innovation of Rama, Parsuram, Krishna, Mohammed, Jesus, Shirdi Sai, Peter, David, Issac, Jacob, Elijah, Moses, John, the modern day food ecosystem have dynamics, association, nanoscule and infinitesimal with equity theory. If non-entity engulfs then with equity Chinnamastaka engulfs with cradle-bath for its every entity, this means it touches the non-entity also with equity. This is the basis of equity theory. Equity theory is applicable to 44 sectors in family, in fathership, in equation, in business in future forecasting models of 44 sectors. Equity theory happens through models of regression analysis, correlation, path models, ANOVA. Equity theory is the basis of leadership and food pyramid creation,growth and innovation and maintenance.

RICH-RAG THEORY/PENNY-PIE FRACTION DEVELOPMENT THEORY

Income = Expenditure + Saving

Light of the word of the Lord is the Messiahnic abundance. Minimal sin maximum production (the scratching of upper surface is sin). The more the money, the more the entity, the more the realization,the more the God. The entity comes with non-entity to kill, steal, damage or destroy. To every action these is equal and opposite reaction. Energy can neither be created nor destroyed. The sum total of energy in this universe is constant. The fear of God is beginning of wisdom. The word of Lord is the daily bread, "hear" for Gospel fortune. Wordly contentment tided, lavished, the Mammon binds (Chains) with tentacles the strata to keep the earth (trouble)makers out to bring Maya,so that only the Lord's name prevails Yeshua, Gautam Buddha and Jagannath. This breakthrough model is fool-proof evidence of Mammon around with heavenly swoosh, and quietness, praise the Lord for the penny-pie. Melting and waking, melting and waiting, ultimately syncing with Godhead reality as nectar-melting,supranormal tricklets in ever-expanding infinitesimal essence of quantascule,Galaxial-drift universe.

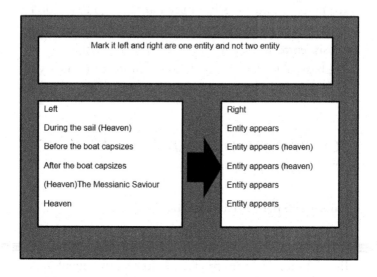

The tools,techniques,stunts,gimmicks,engineered archetype of Mammon,helps in having a smooth sail.Aliens also during Rama's period and during 19th century and ahead millennia worked closely with Mammon in right-capsizing as the light journey is eternal with subtle to delicate to infinitesimal truth of Gospel. Ultimately at each hurdle we have mixed infinitesimal hurdles to undermine our stakes so that Chinnamastaka appears to nullify your point of reference and increases in mega-economica scale,the entity presence,so as to a realized, sound, waiting, messiahnic saviour-call relief and status quo rescued as inbuilt RNA of provision for de Novo cradle bath as a pampered baby with chinnamastaka compassion cushion but cherishing,the presence as absentia as Lord to appear again, again, again giving life force for only uttering the word of Lord as the seasonal saviour as personal lovable infinitesimal geni at work to spread the message of compassion, peace, and Ramayek. Things to repeat the energy as Lord always lits up and nevertheless does shine out giving ultimately resplendent growth of faith, peace, praise to the lord for the hidden Messiahnic outcome pour of bliss and bless as ultimate grains to be cooked and binded by will to nourish the heaven under the sun for a catchment and baby boomer of ideal children, who suck not the fabric but the breathe of the Lord as Lord reigns to bring rain to the kingdom as ultimatum for the truth it received from its children as the last but unending quench of boat sail with the steadfast hand nurturing to show the path of peace bloom. One moment in the presence of Lord purifies you more whiter than snow. You are that meek nature, that pure to see the Lord. The presence of Lord indicates further reducing to point or bundle of whiteness, opening gateways of freedom from bondage-(Space-time)-(material-physicality-healing)-(quantum metaphysics and practical –metaphysics of karma-matter-transcendental threshold vibration or transmutation or transformation) ultimately paving the LORD-LORD pathway, mindset, a charged tuning fork effervescently repeating standards of sweet sound thus ultimately emerging in supreme Godhead. Poverty is a curse, honour God.

Root cause of poverty

LACKING JUST BEING

LACKING LEARNING BEING

LACKING IMPROVE BEING

LACKING CHANGE BEING

Poverty and shame come to him who refuses instruction and correction. He who cultivates his land will have plenty of bread but he who follows worthless people will be trapped in poverty and death. Endurable wealth comes little by little.

Evil thoughts-snake brood

WORRY

CAPTURED

ATTACKED

STATE OF DEPRESSION

Supernatural abundance

God shall declare supernatural abundance for you. The Rawls Distributive Equity is apt before the Lord, as Lord itself is giant infinity. With equity of past, present and future you shall be fond of being gifted with prosperity of wealth and happiness. God is lovable in rewarding you with fullness, plumpness, hale, heartiness of prosperous wealth. God's kingdom is infinite and expands in the realms. God's kingdom is in surety laden with nectareous food, recipes, wealth and the priceless. The image is the proof of getting the vision true. Innate passion is the driver of the machinery by Karmic propoundation. God the master of the world is surely thinking about you. He will bring true sounds of maternal love through abundance i.e for you only as infinite 3-Dimensional shaping of the time –entity and Karma is by God to love all and serve all,so ultimately the abundance battle is won by you by default with God at helm of affairs with natal cords of you in/at womb to feed directly, making supernatural abundance, the rule each now, moment, today, tomorrow, fortnight, week, month, year, second, minute, and hours. The God kingdom is priceless, infinitesimally rich, laden with fortune of the kingly man for every child/ ward of Lord. As the imagination is vivid and rich so also the God's kingdom/words is vivid and richful ornate of the priceless, your good deeds, clean and kind heart and sweet talk would reap your harvests. The self-hypnosis/self-induced of goodness, good deeds, clean and kind heart and sweet talk would reap you to profound Godly rewards of feetwashing in the glory of the Lord. Distributive-Law and reaping dividends of harvest pertains God's divine nature and represents moral attributes. The same miracle is happening today and tomorrow. God is the same "historic" yesterday, today and tomorrow. The same miracle is happening today and tomorrow. Our season of living is to experience God "No men come to Father but through me". God is in our personal lives and our living rooms, opens our doors and gives us lives, because he loves you. The wages of sin is death. Culture rechristened is technology.

TREASURE THE WORDS AND PONDER THEM IN YOUR HEART

BIBLIOGRAPHY

Schmid, Randolph E. .Scientists Confirm Mistake: New. Dinosaur a Combination of Mismatched Fossils. Associated Press. April 7, 2000. Retrieved from http://abcnews.go.com/ sections/science/DailyNews/dino_mistke000407.html.

Scruton, Roger. .Why I Became a Conservative. *The New Criterion*. Retrieved from http://www.newcriterion.com/ archive/21/feb03/burke.htm.

Shalit, Wendy. .A Ladies. Room of One.s Own. *Commentary* 100:2 (August 1995), pp. 33-37.

Moreland, J. P. and William Lane Craig. *Philosophical Foundations for a Christian Worldview.*

Downers Grove, IL: InterVarsity, 2003.

Motluk, Alison. ..Of Moths and Men,. by Judith Hooper. Salon.com Books. Sept. 18, 2002.*Salon.com*. Retrieved from <http://www.salon.com/books/review/2002/09/18/hooper>.

Nash, Ronald H. *Faith and Reason: Searching for a Rational Faith*. Grand Rapids: Zondervan, 1988.

Nash, Ronald H. *Worldviews in Conflict: Choosing Christianity in a World of Ideas*. Grand Rapids:Zondervan, 1992.

Nenon, Tom. .Martin Heidegger. In Richard H. Popkin, ed. *The Columbia History of WesternPhilosophy*. New York: MJF Books, 1999.

.Officials See Rise in Lab Fraud,. Orange County [California] *Register*. January 22, 2003, News 13.

Olasky, Marvin. .Media Christophobia. *World* 17:16 (April 27, 2002). Retrieved from http://www.worldmag.com/world/issue/04-27-02/cover_3.asp.

Olson, Storrs L. Letter to Dr. Peter Raven. November 1, 1999. Retrieved from http://www.answersingenesis.org/docs/4159.asp?vPrint=1.

Pascal, Blaise. *Pensees*. Tr. Martin Turnell. New York: Harper & Row, 1962.

.Paul Ehrlich. *Overpopulation.com*. Retrieved from http://www.overpopulation.com/faq/people/paul_ehrlich.html.

Peterson, Michael. *With All Your Mind: A Christian Philosophy of Education*. Notre Dame:University of Notre Dame, 2001.

Etzioni, Amitai. *The Monochrome Society*. Princeton: Princeton University Press, 2001.

Fennick, John H. *Studies Show: A Popular Guide to Understanding Scientific Studies*. New York:Prometheus Books, 1997.

Feyerabend, Paul. *Against Method*. London: NLB, 1975.

Feyerabend, Paul. *Paul K. Feyerabend: Knowledge, Science, and Relativism, Philosophical Papers*. Vol.3. Ed. John Preston. Cambridge: Cambridge University Press, 1999.

Fine, Gary Alan. .The Ten Commandments of Writing. *The American Sociologist*. Summer 199819:2 152-157.

Fischer, David Hackett. *Historians. Fallacies: Toward a Logic of Historical Thought*. New York:Harper & Row, 1970.

Fonte, John. .Why There Is a Culture War. *Policy Review* 104, Dec. 2000-Jan. 2001), pp. 15-31.

Fraser, David. .Book Summary Notes on David Gill, *The Opening of the Christian Mind: TakingEvery Thought Captive to Christ*. In *Discipleship and the Disciplines: Enhancing Faith-Learning Integration*. Coalition for Christian Colleges and Universities, 1996.

Davis, Edward B. .Some Comments on the Course, .Introduction to Christianity and Science... Retrieved online at <http://www.messiah.edu/hpages/facstaff/davis/course.html>.

DeLashmutt, Gary and Roger Braund,.Postmodern Impact: Education. In Dennis McCallum,ed., *The Death of Truth.* Minneapolis: Bethany House, 1996.

Dembski, William. *Intelligent Design: The Bridge Between Science and Theology.* Downers Grove, IL:InterVarsity, 1999.

Dixon, Tom. .Postmodern Method: History. In Dennis McCallum, ed. *The Death of Truth.*Minneapolis: Bethany House, 1996.

D.Souza, Dinesh. *Illiberal Education: The Politics of Race and Sex on Campus.* New York: The FreePress, 1991.

D.Souza, Dinesh. *The End of Racism: Principles for a Multiracial Society.* New York: The Free Press,1995.

Dupre, Louis. .Postmodernity or Late Modernity? Ambiguities in Richard Rorty.s Thought. *TheReview of Metaphysics* 47:2 (Dec. 1993), pp. 277-296.

Easterbrook, Greg. .Science Sees the Light. *The New Republic* 219:15 (Oct. 12, 1998), pp. 24-30.

Eger, Martin. .A Tale of Two Controversies: Dissonance in the Theory and Practice ofRationality. Zygon 23:3 (September 1988), pp. 291-325.

Eliot, T. S. *Christianity and Culture: The Idea of a Christian Society and Notes Towards the Definition ofCulture.* New York: Harcourt, 1948.

Ellis, Frank. .Political Correctness and the Ideological Struggle: From Lenin and Mao to Marcuseand Foucault. *Journal of Social, Political, and Economic Studies* 27:4 (Winter 2002), pp. 409-444.

Ellis, John M. *Against Deconstruction*. Princeton, NJ: Princeton U. Press, 1989.

Gilder, George. .The Materialist Superstition. *Intercollegiate Review* 21:2 (Spring 1996), pp. 6-14.

Gill, David. *The Opening of the Christian Mind: Taking Every Thought Captive to Christ*. DownersGrove, IL: InterVarsity, 1989.

Goldberg, Bernard. *Bias: A CBS Insider Exposes How the Media Distort the News*. Washington, D.C.:Regnery, 2002.

Greidanus, Sidney. .The Use of the Bible in Christian Scholarship. *Christian Scholar.s Review* 11:2(March 1982), pp. 138-147.

Groothuis, Douglas. .Defenders of the Faith. *Books and Culture*, July-August 2003,.

THE INTEGRATION OF FAITH AND LEARNING

Harris, Trester S. Patients Are People, Too. *VirtualSalt*. Retrieved from http://www.virtualsalt.com/pp/.

Hasker, William. .Faith-Learning Integration: An Overview. *Christian Scholars Review* 21:3(March 1992), pp. 231-248.

Retrieved online at <http://www.gospelcom.net/journals/csr/hasker.html>.

Hasker, William. *Metaphysics: Constructing a World View.* Downers Grove, IL: InterVarsity, 1983.

Haughness, Norman and Thomas W. Clark. .Postmodern Anti-Foundationalism Examined. *TheHumanist* July-Aut 1993, pp. 19-22.

Heath, Peter. *The Philosopher.s Alice.* New York: St. Martin.s, 1974.

Hecht, Jeff. .F Is for Fake. *New Scientist.* Feb. 19, 2000, p. 12.

Himmelfarb, Gertrude. The Christian University: A Call to Counterrevolution. *Discipleship andthe Disciplines: Enhancing Faith-Learning Integration.* Coalition for Christian Colleges andUniversities, 1996.

Paul Marshall and Lela Gilbert, Heaven is Not my Home: Learning to Live in God's Creation (Nashville: Word Publishing, 1998).

Gilbert C. Meilander, ed., Working: Its Meaning and Its Limits (Notre Dame, Notre DameUniversity Press, 2000).

David W. Miller, God at Work: The History and Promise of the Faith at Work Movement (Oxford University Press, 2006).

Paul Minear, "Work and Vocation in Scripture," in J. Nelson, ed., Work and Vocation (New York: Harper, 1954).

Bruce Nicholls, Contextualization: A Theology of Gospel and Culture (Downers Grove: InterVarsity Press, 1979).

Kathleen Norris, Acedia & Me: A Marriage, Monks, and a Writer's Life (New York: Penguin Books, 2008).

Michael Novak, Business as a Calling: Work and the Examined Life (New York: The Free Press, 1996).

Michael Novak, Toward a Theology of the Corporation (Washington: American Enterprise Institute for Public Policy Research, 1982).

William Perkins, "A Treatise of the Vocations or Callings of Men" in The Work of William Perkins, ed. and intro. By Ian Breward (Appleford, UK: Courtenay Press, 1970).

Gordon Preece, Changing Work Values: A Christian Response (Melbourne: Acorn Press, 1995).

Alan Richardson, The Biblical Doctrine of Work (London: SCM Press, 1954).

Jeremy Rifkin, The End of Work: The Decline of the Global Work-Force and the Dawn of the Post-Market Era (London: Penguin Books, 2000).

Leland Ryken, Redeeming the Time: A Christian Approach to Work and Leisure (Grand Rapids; Baker, 1995).

Jeffrey Salkin, Being God's Partner: How to Find the Hidden Link Between Spirituality and Your Work (Woodstock, Vermont: Jewish Lights Publishing, 1994).

Doug Sherman and William Hendricks, Your Work Matters to God (Colorado Springs, Navpress, 1987).

Stephen R. Graves and Thomas G. Addington, The Fourth Frontier: Exploring the New World of Work (Nashville: Word, 2000).

Mark Greene, The Great Divide (London: The London Institute for Contemporary Christianity, 2010).

Thomas H. Green, Darkness in the Marketplace: The Christian at Prayer in the World (Notre Dame, Ind.: Ave Maria Press, 1981).

R. Greenleaf, Servant Leadership (NJ.: Paulist Press, 1977).

Brian Griffiths, The Creation of Wealth (London: Hodder and Stoughton, 1984).

Os Guiness, The Call: Finding and Fulfilling the Central Purpose of Your Life (Nashville: Word, 1998).

Pete Hammond, R. Paul Stevens and Todd Svanoe, The Marketplace Annotated Bibliography: A Christian Guide to Books on Work, Business and Vocation (Downers Grove: InterVarsity Press, 2002).

Lee Hardy, The Fabric of This World: Inquiries into Calling, Career Choice and the Design of Human Work (Grand Rapids: Eerdmans, 2006).

John Haughey, Converting Nine to Five: A Spirituality of Daily Work (New York: Crossroad, 1989).

S. Helgesen, The Female Advantage: Women's Ways of Leadership (New York: Doubleday, 1990).

Donald R. Heiges, The Christian's Calling (Philadelphia: United Lutheran Church in America, 1958).

Dennis W. Bakke, Joy at Work: A Revolutionary Approach to Fun on the Job (Toronto: Viking Canada, 2005).

Ray Bakke, Lowell Bakke and William Hendricks, Joy at Work Bible Study Companion (PVC: www.dennisbakke.com).

Robert Banks, God the Worker: Journeys into the Mind, Heart and Imagination of God (Valley Forge: Judson Press, 1994).

Robert Banks & Kimberly Powell, eds., Faith in Leadership: How Leaders Live Out Their Faith in Their Work and Why It Matters (San Francisco: Jossey-Bass, 2000).

John D. Beckett, Loving Monday: Succeeding in Business without Losing Your Soul _____, Mastering Monday: A Guide to Integrating Faith and Work (Downers Grove: InterVarsity Press, 2006).

John A. Bernbaum and Simon Steer, Why Work? Careers and Employment in Biblical Perspective (Grand Rapids: Baker Book House, 1986).

Peter L. Berstein, Against the Gods: The Remarkable Story of Risk (New York: John Wiley and Sons, 1996).

Peter Block, Stewardship: Choosing Service Over Self (Koehler, 1995).

Yves Congar, Lay People in the Church: A Study for a Theology of the Laity, Trans. D. Attwater (Westminster MD.: Newman Press, 1957).

Robert Farrar Capon, An Offering of Uncles: The Priesthood of Adam and the Shape of the World (New York: Crossroad, 1982).

Darrell Cosden, The Heavenly Good of Earthly Work (Peabody, Mass.: Hendrickson, 2006).

_____, A Theology of Work: Work and the New Creation (Carlisle, Cumbria, UK: Paternoster Press, 2004).

John Dalla Costa, Magnificence at Work: Living Faith in Business (Ottawa: Saint Paul University – Novalis Press, 2005).

Matthew B. Crawford, Shop Class As Soul Craft: An Inquiry into the Value of Work (New York: Penguin Press, 2009).

109

Andrew Crouch, Culture Making: Recovering our Creative Calling (Downers Grove: intervarsity Press, 2008).

Peter Curran, All the Hours God Sends? Practical and Biblical Help in Meeting the Demands of Work (Leicester, UK: InterVarsity Press, 2000).

Alain de Bottom, The Pleasures and Sorrows of Work (New York: Pantheon Books, 2009).

William E. Diehl, Thank God It's Monday (Philadelphia: Fortress Press,1982).

_____ _, The Monday Connection: A Spirituality of Competence, Affirmation, and Support in the Workplace (San Francisco: HarperSanFrancisco, 1991).

William E. Diehl and Judith Ruhe Diehl, It Ain't Over Till It's Over (Minneapolis: Augsburg Books, 2003).

William L. Droel, Business People: The Spirituality of Work (Chicago: ACTA Publications, 1990).

William Dumbrell, "Creation, Covenant and Work," Crux 24, no. 3 (September 1988): 14-24.

Robert M. Grant, "Work and Occupations," in Early Christianity and Society (New York: Harper & Row Publishers, 1977).

Richard Higginson, Questions of Business Life: Exploring Workplace Issues from a Christian Perspective (Carlisle, Cumbria, UK: Spring Harvest, 2002).

_____, Called to Account: Adding Value in God's World: Integrating Christianity and Business Effectively (Glasgow: HarperCollins, 1993).

R. F. Hock, The Social Context of Paul's Ministry: Tentmaking and Apostleship (Philadelphia: Fortress Press, 1980).

Joe Holland, Creative Communion: Toward a Spirituality of Work (Mahwah, NJ: Paulist Press, 1989).

D.H. Jenson, Responsive Labor: A Theology of Work (Louisville: Westminster Kohn Knox Press, 2006).

Barbara Killinger, Workaholics: The Respectable Addicts (New York: Simon and Schuster, 1991).

Robert Henderson,Unlocking destinies from courts of Heaven: Robert Henderson Ministries,August 30 2016.

Joyce Meyer,Battlefield of the Mind - Feasting at the King's Table:

Joyce Meyer Ministries,New York Boston Nashville., ·2009

Patricia King,SpiritualRevolution_Experiences:Patricia King ministries 96Pages· 2013

Joseph Prince,GOSPELREVOLUTION: Joseph Prince Ministries· 2012

Andrew-Wommack,Spirit-Soul-Body: Andrew Wommack ministries 2012·

Creflo A. Dollar Live Without Fear: Learn to Walk in God's Power and Peace Kindle Edition

Daniel Kolenda,Unlocking The Miraculous, Kindle Edition

Hendrik Kraemer, A Theology of the Laity (Philadelphia: Westminster Press, 1958).

Armand Larive, After Sunday: A Theology of Work (New York: Continuum, 2004).

Paul Marshall, A Kind of Life Imposed on Man: Vocation and Social Order from Tyndale to Locke (Toronto: University of Toronto Press, 1996).

_____, Thine Is the Kingdom (Grand Rapids: Eerdmans, 1986).

Alexander Schmemann, For the Life of the World (Crestwood, NY: St. Vladimir's Seminary Press, 1988).

Michael Young and Tom Schuller, Life After Work: The Arrival of the Ageless Society (London: Harper Collins, 1991).

Christopher Schumacher, God in Work: Discovering the Divine Pattern for Work in the New Millenium (Oxford, Lion Publishing, 1998).

Max L. Stackhouse, God and Globalization: Religion and the Common Powers of Life, Volume 1(T&T Clark International, 2000).

R. Paul Stevens, The Other Six Days: Vocation, Work and Ministry in Biblical Perspective (Grand Rapids: Eerdmans, 1999),published in UK under the title: The Abolition of the Laity

_____, Down-to-Earth Spirituality: Encountering God in the Ordinary, Boring Stuff of Life (Downers Grove: InterVarsity Press, 2003).

_____, Doing God's Business: Meaning and Motivation for the Marketplace

_____, "The Spiritual & Religious Sources of Entrepreneurship: From Max Weber to the New Business Spirituality, Crux, Vol XXXVI, No 2 (June 2000), 22-33; reprinted in Stimulus: The New Zealand Journal of Christian Thought and Practice, Vol 9, Issues 1 (Feb 2001):2-11.

R. Paul Stevens and Robert Banks, Marketplace Ministry Handbook (Vancouver: Regent College Publishing, 2005).

R. Paul Stevens and Alvin Ung, Taking Your Soul to Work: Overcoming the Nine Deadly Sins in the Workplace (Grand Rapids: Eerdmans, 2010).

Benny Tabalujian, God on Monday: Reflections on Christians @ Work (Melbourne, Australia: Klesis Institute, 2005).

Reg Theriault, How to Tell When You're Tired: A Brief Examination of Work (New York: W.W. Norton& Co., 1995).

Studs Terkel, Working: People Talk About What They Do All Day and How They Feel About What They Do (New York: Ballantine Books, 1974).

John Ting, Living Biblically at Work (Singapore: Landmark Books. 1995).

Paul Tournier, The Gift of Feeling, trans. Edwin Hudson (Atlanta: John Knox Press, 1979).

Gene E. Veith, God at Work: Your Christian Vocation in All of Life (Wheaton: Crossway, 2002). Miroslav Volf, Work in the Spirit: Toward a Theology of Work (New York: Oxford University Press, 1991).

_____, "Human Work, Divine Spirit, and the New Creation: Toward a Pneumatological Understanding of Work," Pneuma: The Journal of the Society for Pentecostal Studies (Fall 1987): 173-193.

Ben Witherington III, Work: A Kingdom Perspective on Labor (Grand Rapids: Eerdmans, 2011).

Stefan Cardinal Wyszynski, All You Who Labor: Work and the Sanctification of Daily Life (Manchester, NH: Sophia Institute Press, 1995).

Alfred, Jay. Between the Moon and Earth. Victoria, BC: Trafford Publishing, 2006.

———. Brains and Realities. Victoria, BC: Trafford Publishing, 2006.

———. Our Invisible Bodies: Scientific Evidence for Subtle Bodies. Victoria, BC: Trafford Publishing, 2006.

Aspden, Harold. Modern Aether Science. Southampton, UK: Sabberton Publications, 1972.

Bartlett, Richard. Matrix Energetics: The Science and Art of Transformation. Hillsboro, OR: Atria Books/Beyond Words, 2007.

Bearden, Thomas E. AIDS Biological Warfare. Greenville, TX: Tesla Book Company, 1988.

———. Excalibur Briefing: Explaining Paranormal Phenomena. Santa Barbara, CA: Cheniere, 2002.

———. Energy from the Vacuum: Concepts and Principles. Santa Barbara, CA: Cheniere, 2002.

———. Oblivion: America at the Brink. Santa Barbara, CA: Cheniere, 2005.

———. Fer de Lance. Santa Barbara, CA: Cheniere, 2003.

———. Gravitobiology: A New Biophysics. Santa Barbara, CA: Cheniere, 2003.

Bedini, John, and Thomas Bearden. Free Energy Generation—Circuits and Schematics: 20 Bedini-Bearden Years. Santa Barbara, CA: Cheniere, 2006.

Bentov, Itzhak. Stalking the Wild Pendulum: On the Mechanics of Consciousness. Rochester, VT: Destiny Books, 1988.

———. A Brief Tour of Higher Consciousness: A Cosmic Book on the Mechanics of Creation. Rochester, VT: Destiny Books, 2006.

Cathie, Bruce L. The Harmonic Conquest of Space. Kempton, IL: Adventures Unlimited, 1998.

———. The Energy Grid. Kempton, IL: Adventures Unlimited, 1997.

Cheney, Margaret. Tesla: Man Out of Time. New York: Barnes & Noble Books, 1993.

Childress, David Hatcher. Anti-Gravity and the Unified Field. Kempton, IL: Adventures Unlimited, 2001.

———. The Time Travel Handbook: A Manual of Practical Teleportation and Time Travel. Kempton, IL: Adventures Unlimited, 1999.

Chopra, Deepak. The Third Jesus: The Christ We Cannot Ignore. New York: Harmony, 2008.

Coats, Callum. Living Energies: An Exposition of Concepts Related to the Theories of Viktor Schauberger. Dublin, Ireland: Gateway Books, 2001.

Cook, Nick. The Hunt for Zero Point: One Man's Journey to Discover the Biggest Secret Since the Invention of the Atom Bomb. London: Century, 2001.

Dalal, A. S. Powers Within. Pondicherry, India: Sri Aurobindo Ashram Publications Department, 1999.

Deary, Terry. Vanished! Boston: Kingfisher, 2004.

Dennett, Preston. Human Levitation: A True History and How-to Manual. Grand Rapids, MI: Schiffer Publishing, 2006.

Dolley, Chris. Shift. Riverdale, NY: Baen Books, 2007.

Dowling, Levi. The Aquarian Gospel of Jesus the Christ. New York: Cosimo Classics, 2007.

Dunn, Christopher. The Giza Power Plant: Technologies of Ancient Egypt. Rochester, VT: Bear & Company, 1998.

Durr, Hans-Peter, Fritz-Albert Popp, and Wolfram Schommers. What Is Life? Scientific Approaches and Philosophical Positions. Hackensack, NJ: World Scientific, 2002.

Edwards, Harry. Harry Edwards: Thirty Years a Spiritual Healer. Surrey, UK: Jenkins, 1968.

Farrell, Joseph P. The Cosmic War: Interplanetary Warfare, Modern Physics, and Ancient Texts. Kempton, IL: Adventures Unlimited, 2007.

————. The Giza Death Star Deployed: The Physics and Engineering of the Great Pyramid. Kempton, IL: Adventures Unlimited, 2003.

————. The Giza Death Star Destroyed: The Ancient War for Future Science. Kempton, IL: Adventures Unlimited, 2005.

————. Reich of the Black Sun: Nazi Secret Weapons & the Cold War Allied Legend. Kempton, IL: Adventures Unlimited, 2005.

————. Secrets of the Unified Field: The Philadelphia Experiment, the Nazi Bell, and the Discarded Theory. Kempton, IL: Adventures Unlimited, 2008.

————. The SS Brotherhood of the Bell: The Nazis' Incredible Secret Technology. Kempton, IL: Adventures Unlimited, 2006.

Friedman, Norman. The Hidden Domain: Home of the Quantum Wave Function, Nature's Creative Source. Eugene, OR: Woodbridge Group, 1997.

Garrison, Cal. Slim Spurling's Universe: The Light-Life Technology: Ancient Science Rediscovered to Restore the Health of the Environment and Mankind. Frederick, CO: IX-EL Publishing, 2004.

Green, Glenda. The Keys of Jeshua. Sedona, AZ: Spiritis Publishing, 2004.

Harbison, W. A. Projekt UFO: The Case for Man-made Flying Saucers. Charleston, SC: BookSurge, 2007.

Harpur, Patrick. Daimonic Reality: A Field Guide to the Otherworld. Ravens-dale, WA: Pine Winds, 2003.

Ho, Mae-Wan. The Rainbow and the Worm: The Physics of Organisms. Hack-ensack, NJ: World Scientific, 1998.

Hoagland, Richard C., and Mike Bara. Dark Mission: The Secret History of NASA. Los Angeles: Feral House, 2007.

James, John. The Great Field: Soul at Play in a Conscious Universe. Fulton, CA: Energy Psychology Press, 2008.

King, Moray B. The Energy Machine of T. Henry Moray: Zero-Point Energy & Pulsed Plasma Physics. Kempton, IL: Adventures Unlimited, 2005.

Knight, Christopher, and Alan Butler. Who Built the Moon? London: Watkins Publishing, 2005.

Kraft, Dean. A Touch of Hope: A Hands-On Healer Shares the Miraculous Power of Touch. New York: Berkley Trade, 1998.

Kron, Gabriel. Tensors for Circuits. New York: Dover Publications, 1959.

Laszlo, Ervin. Science and the Akashic Field: An Integral Theory of Everything. Rochester, VT: Inner Traditions, 2004.

———. Science and the Reenchantment of the Cosmos: The Rise of the Integral Vision of Reality. Rochester, VT: Inner Traditions, 2006.

LaViolette, Paul A. Genesis of the Cosmos: The Ancient Science of Continuous Creation. Rochester, VT: Bear & Company, 2004.

———. Secrets of Antigravity Propulsion: Tesla, UFOs, and Classified Aerospace Technology. Rochester, VT: Bear & Company, 2008.

———. Subquantum Kinetics: A Systems Approach to Physics and Cosmology. Alexandria, VA: Starlane Publications, 2003.

Lilly, John C. The Scientist: A Metaphysical Autobiography. Oakland, CA: Ronin Publishing, 1996.

Lloyd, Seth. Programming the Universe: A Quantum Computer Scientist Takes on the Cosmos. London: Vintage Books, 2007.

Lyne, William R. Pentagon Aliens. Lamy, NM: Creatopia Productions, 1999.

Maxwell, James Clerk. An Elementary Treatise on Electricity. Mineola, NY: Dover Publications, 2005.

Monroe, Robert A. Journeys Out of the Body. Garden City, NY: Anchor, 1977.

Moore, William, and Charles Berlitz. The Philadelphia Experiment: Project Invisibility. New York: Fawcett, 1995.

Murakami, Aaron C. The Quantum Key. Seattle: White Dragon, 2007.

Oschman, James L. Energy Medicine: The Scientific Basis. New York: Churchill Livingstone, 2000.

Pickover, Clifford A. Sex, Drugs, Einstein, and Elves: Sushi, Psychedelics, Parallel Universes, and the Quest for Transcendence. Petaluma, CA: Smart Publications, 2005.

Popp, Fritz Albert, and L. V. Belousov. Integrative Biophysics: Biophotonics. New York: Springer, 2003.

Prophet, Mark L., and Elizabeth Clare Prophet. Saint Germain on Alchemy: Formulas for Self-Transformation. Livingston, MT: Summit University, 1993.

Randles, Jenny. Time Travel: Fact, Fiction & Possibility. New York: Blandford Press, 1994.

Regardie, Israel. The Golden Dawn: The Original Account of the Teachings, Rites & Ceremonies of the Hermetic Order. St. Paul, MN: Llewellyn Publications, 1986.

Richards, Steve. Invisibility: Mastering the Art of Vanishing. Wellingborough, UK: Aquarian Press, 1982.

Rothman, Tony. Everything's Relative: And Other Fables from Science and Technology. Hoboken, NJ: John Wiley & Sons, 2003.

Rothman, Tony, and George Sudarshan. Doubt and Certainty. Reading, MA: Helix Books, 1998.

Russell, Edward W. Report on Radionics: The Science Which Can Cure Where Orthodox Medicine Fails. Essex, UK: C. W. Daniel, 1973.

Russell, Ronald, and Charles T. Tart. The Journey of Robert Monroe: From Out-of-Body Explorer to Consciousness Pioneer. Charlottesville, VA: Hampton Roads Publishing, 2007.

Samanta-Laughton, Manjir. Punk Science: Inside the Mind of God. Ropley, Hants, UK: O Books, 2006.

Sheldrake, Rupert. The Presence of the Past: Morphic Resonance and the Habits of Nature. Rochester, VT: Park Street, 1988.

Scheinfeld, Robert. Busting Loose from the Money Game. Hoboken, NJ: Wiley, 2006.

Strauss, Michael. Requiem for Relativity: The Collapse of Special Relativity. Pembroke Pines, FL: RelativityCollapse. com, 2004.

Sussman, Janet I. Timeshift: The Experience of Dimensional Change. Fairfield, IA: Time Portal Publications, 1996.

Swanson, Claude. The Synchronized Universe: New Science of the Paranormal. Tucson, AZ: Poseidia Press, 2003.

Talbot, Michael. Mysticism and the New Physics. New York: Penguin, 1993.

Tansley, David V. Radionics Interface with the Ether Fields. Boston: C. W. Daniel, 1975.

Tiller, William A. Science and Human Transformation: Subtle Energies, Intentionality, and Consciousness. Walnut Creek, CA: Pavior Publishing, 1997.

Tiller, William A., Walter Dibble, and Gregory J. Fandel. Some Science Adventures with Real Magic. Walnut Creek, CA: Pavior Publishing, 2005.

Tiller, William A., Walter Dibble, and Michael Kohane. Conscious Acts of Creation: The Emergence of a New Physics. Walnut Creek, CA: Pavior Publishing, 2001.

Valone, Thomas F. Electrogravitics II: Validating Reports on a New Propulsion Methodology. Washington, DC: Integrity Research Institute, 2000.

———. Harnessing the Wheelwork of Nature: Tesla's Science of Energy. Kempton, IL: Adventures Unlimited, 2002.

———. Practical Conversion of Zero-Point Energy: Feasibility Study of the Extraction of Zero-Point Energy from the Quantum Vacuum for the Performance of Useful Work. 3rd ed. Beltsville, MD: Integrity Research Institute, 2003.

———. Zero Point Energy: The Fuel of the Future. Beltsville, MD: Integrity Research Institute, 2007.

Valone, Thomas F., and Elizabeth A. Rausher. Electrogravitics Systems: Reports on a New Propulsion Methodology. Washington, DC: Integrity Research Institute, 2001.

Violette, John R. Extra-Dimensional Universe: Where the Paranormal Becomes Normal. Charlottesville, VA: Hampton Roads, 2005.

Wang, Robert. The Qabalistic Tarot: A Textbook of Mystical Philosophy. Columbia, MD: Marcus Aurelius Press, 2004.

Wesson, Paul S. Five-Dimensional Physics: Classical and Quantum Consequences of Kaluza-Klein Cosmology. Hackensack, NJ: World Scientific, 2006.

Yogananda, Paramahansa. The Second Coming of Christ: The Resurrection of the Christ Within You. Los Angeles: Self-Realization Fellowship, 2004.

———. Self-Realization. Los Angeles: Self-Realization Fellowship, 2004.

———. The Yoga of Jesus: Understanding the Hidden Teachings of the Gospels. Los Angeles: Self-Realization Fellowship, 2007.

Anderson, Stephen R. Doctor Dolittle's Delusion: Animals and the Uniqueness of Human Language. New Haven, CT: Yale University Press, 2004.

Beth, Evert W. The Foundations of Mathematics: A Study in the Philosophy of Science. 2nd rev. ed. Amsterdam: North-Holland, 1968.

Bishop, Steve. "A Bibliography for a Christian Approach to Mathematics" (June 7, 2008). http://www.scribd.com/doc/3268416/A -bibliography-for -a -Christian -approach -to -mathematics. Accessed September 17, 2012.

Bradley, James, and Russell Howell. Mathematics through the Eyes of Faith. New York: HarperOne, 2011.

Byl, John. The Divine Challenge: On Matter, Mind, Math, and Meaning. Edinburgh/Carlisle, PA: Banner of Truth, 2004.

Chase, Gene, and Calvin Jongsma. "Bibliography of Christianity and Mathematics, 1st edition 1983." http:// www. asa3.org /ASA /topics /Mathematics /1983 Bibliography. html. Accessed July 30, 2012. This bibliography was published by Dordt College Press in 1983, but is now out of print.

Frame, John M. Apologetics to the Glory of God: An Introduction. Phillipsburg, NJ: Presbyterian & Reformed, 1994.

———. The Doctrine of God. Phillipsburg, NJ: Presbyterian & Reformed, 2002.

———. The Doctrine of the Christian Life. Phillipsburg, NJ: Presbyterian & Reformed, 2008.

———. The Doctrine of the Knowledge of God. Phillipsburg, NJ: Presbyterian & Reformed, 1987.

———. The Doctrine of the Word of God. Phillipsburg, NJ: Presbyterian & Reformed, 2010.

———. Perspectives on the Word of God: An Introduction to Christian Ethics. Eugene, OR: Wipf & Stock, 1999.

Horsten, Leon. "Philosophy of Mathematics." The Stanford Encyclopedia of Philosophy (Spring 2014 Edition). Edited by Edward N. Zalta. http:// plato.stanford.edu /archives /

spr2014 /entries /philosophy -mathematics/. Accessed June 18, 2014.

Howell, Russell W., and W. James Bradley, eds. Mathematics in a Postmodern Age: A Christian Perspective. Grand Rapids, MI/Cambridge: Eerdmans, 2001.

Iemhoff, Rosalie. "Intuitionism in the Philosophy of Mathematics." The Stanford Encyclopedia of Philosophy (Spring 2014 Edition). Edited by Edward N. Zalta. http://plato.stanford.edu /archives /spr2014 /entries/intuitionism/. Accessed June 18, 2014.

Jech, Thomas. "Set Theory." The Stanford Encyclopedia of Philosophy (Winter 2011 Edition). Edited by Edward N. Zalta. http://plato.stanford.edu/archives/win2011/entries/set -theory/.Accessed June 18, 2014.

Kuyk, Willem. Complementarity in Mathematics: A First Introduction to the Foundations of Mathematics and Its History. Dordrecht-Holland/Boston: Reidel, 1977.

Kuyper, Abraham. Lectures on Calvinism: Six Lectures Delivered at Princeton University under Auspices of the L. P. Stone Foundation. Grand Rapids, MI: Eerdmans, 1931.

Meek, Esther L. Longing to Know: The Philosophy of Knowledge for Ordinary People. Grand Rapids, MI: Brazos, 2003.

Milbank, John. The Word Made Strange: Theology, Language, Culture. Oxford: Blackwell, 1997.

Nickel, James. Mathematics: Is God Silent? Rev. ed. Vallecito, CA: Ross, 2001.

Poythress, Vern S. "A Biblical View of Mathematics." In Foundations of Christian Scholarship: Essays in the Van Til Perspective. Edited by Gary North. Vallecito, CA: Ross, 1976. Pp. 158–188. http:// www.frame -poythress. org /a -biblical -view -of -mathematics/. Accessed December 29, 2012.

Bibliography 189

———. God-Centered Biblical Interpretation. Phillipsburg, NJ: Presbyterian & Reformed, 1999.

———. Inerrancy and Worldview: Answering Modern Challenges to the Bible. Wheaton, IL: Crossway, 2012.

———. Logic: A God-Centered Approach to the Foundation of Western Thought. Wheaton, IL: Crossway, 2013.

———. "Mathematics as Rhyme." Journal of the American Scientific Affiliation 35/4 (1983): 196–203.

———. "Newton's Laws as Allegory." Journal of the American Scientific Affiliation 35/3 (1983): 156–161. http:// www.frame -poythress.org /newtons-laws -as -allegory/. Accessed June 18, 2014.

———. Redeeming Philosophy: A God-Centered Approach to the Big Questions. Wheaton, IL: Crossway, 2014.

———. Redeeming Science: A God-Centered Approach. Wheaton, IL: Crossway, 2006.

———. "Science as Allegory." Journal of the American Scientific Affiliation 35/2 (1983): 65–71. http:// www.frame-poythress.org/science-as-allegory/. Accessed June 18, 2014.

———. The Shadow of Christ in the Law of Moses. Phillipsburg, NJ: Presbyterian & Reformed, 1995.

———. Symphonic Theology: The Validity of Multiple Perspectives in Theology. Reprint. Phillipsburg, NJ: Presbyterian & Reformed, 2001.

———. "Tagmemic Analysis of Elementary Algebra." Semiotica 17/2 (1976): 131–151.

Sayers, Dorothy. The Mind of the Maker. New York: Harcourt, Brace, 1941.

Strauss, D. F. M. "The Concept of Number: Multiplicity and Succession between Cardinality and Ordinality," South African Journal of Philosophy 25/1 (2006): 27–47, http://www.freewebs.com/dfmstrauss/Ordinality_and Cardinality .pdf, accessed August 5, 2014.

———. "Frege's Attack on 'Abstraction' and His Defense of the 'Applicability' of Arithmetic (as Part of Logic)," South African Journal of Philosophy 22/1 (2003): 63–80.

———. "Infinity and Continuity: The Mutual Dependence and Distinctness of Multiplicity and Wholeness," paper presented at the Free University of

Brussels, October 15, 2006. http:// www.reformational publishing project.com /rpp /docs /Infinity and Continuity .pdf, accessed August 5, 2014.

———. "The Significance of Non-Reductionist Ontology for the Discipline of Mathematics: A Historical and Systematic Analysis," *Axiomathes* 20 (2010): 19–52. DOI 10.1007/s10516-009-9080-5, http:// link .springer.com / article /10.1007 %2 Fs10 5 1 6 -009 -9080 -5 # page-1, accessed August 5, 2014.

———. "What Is a Line?" *Axiomathes* 24/2 (2014): 181–205.

van Atten, Mark. "Luitzen Egbertus Jan Brouwer." *The Stanford Encyclopedia of Philosophy (Summer 2011 Edition)*. Edited by Edward N. Zalta. http://plato.stanford.edu / archives /sum2011 /entries /brouwer/. Accessed June 18, 2014.

Van Til, Cornelius. *The Defense of the Faith.* 2nd ed., rev. and abridged. Philadelphia: Presbyterian & Reformed, 1963.

Vollenhoven, Dirk H. Theodoor. "Problemen en richtingen in de wijsbegeerte der wiskunde" [Problems and Directions in the Philosophy of Mathematics]. *Philosophia Reformata* 1 (1936): 162–187.

————. *De wijsbegeerte der wiskunde van theïstisch standpunt* [The Philosophy of Mathematics from a Theistic Standpoint]. Amsterdam: Van Soest,1918.

Whitehead, Alfred North, and Bertrand Russell. *Principia Mathematica*. 2nd ed. 3 vols. Cambridge: Cambridge University Press, 1927.

Adler, Mortimer and Charles Van Doren. *How to Read a Book*. Rev. ed. New York: MJF Books,1972.

.Ads Accuse Democrats of Barring Catholics from Bench. *Orange County Register*. July 24, 2003,News 9.

Allan, Kenneth and Jonathan H. Turner. .A Formalization of Postmodern Theory. *SociologicalPerspectives* 43:3, pp. 363-385.

Aristotle. *Nicomachean* Ethics. Tr. Martin Ostwald. New York: Bobbs-Merrill, 1962.

.ASNE Survey: Journalists Say They.re Liberal. *The American Editor*. 26 May 1999. American Society of Newspaper Editors. <http://www.asne.org/kiosk/editor/ 97.janfeb/ dennis4.htm>.

Bacon, Francis. *The New Organon*. 1620. Reprint Indianapolis: Bobbs-Merrill, 1960.

Behe, Michael. *Darwin.s Black Box: The Biochemical Challenge to Evolution*. New York: Free Press,1996.

Bengtsson, Jan Olof. .Left and Right Eclecticism: Roger Kimball.s Cultural Criticism. *Humanitas*14:1 (2001), pp. 23-46.

Bennett, William J. *The De-Valuing of America: The Fight for Our Culture and Our Children*. NewYork: Summit, 1992.

Berlinski, David. .A Scientific Scandal? David Berlinski and Critics. *Commentary*. Retrieved fromhttp://www.commentary.org/berlinski.htm.

Boa, Kenneth D. and Robert M. Bowman. *Faith Has Its Reasons: An Integrative Approach toDefending Christianity*. Colorado Springs: NavPress, 2001.

Broad, William and Nicholas Wade. *Betrayers of the Truth: Fraud and Deceit in the Halls of Science*.New York: Simon and Schuster, 1982.

Brother Lawrence. *The Practice of the Presence of God*. Tr. Donald Atwater. Springfield, IL:Templegate, 1974.

Carr, David. .Husserl and Phenomenology. In Richard H. Popkin, ed. *The Columbia History ofWestern Philosophy*. New York: MJF Books, 1999.

.Darwinism: A Time for Funerals. *Contrast*. March-April 1983, pp. 4-5. Himmelfarb, Gertrude. *Darwin and the Darwinian Revolution*. New York: W. W. Norton, 1962.

Hoffmann, Roald. .Why Buy That Theory?. *American Scientist* 91:1 (Jan-Feb 2003), pp. 9-11.

Hollander, Paul. .Marxism and Western Intellectuals in the Post-Communist Era. *Society* 37:2(Jan-Feb 2000), pp. 22-28.

Hooper, Judith. *Of Moths and Men: The Untold Story of Science and the Peppered Moth.* New York: W.W. Norton, 2002.

Horowitz, David. .Missing Diversity on America.s Campuses. *FrontPageMagazine.com*, Sept. 3,2002. Retrieved from http://www.frontpagemag.com/articles/Printable. asp?ID=1003.

Huxley, Aldous. *Ends and Means: An Inquiry into the Nature of Ideals and into the Methods Employedfor Their Realization.* New York: Harper, 1937.

Iannone, Carol. .PC with a Human Face. *Commentary* 96:6 (June 1993), pp. 44-48.

Iannone, Carol. .Sex and the Feminists. *Commentary* 96:3 (September 1993), pp. 51-54.

Ingram, David. .Continental Philosophy: Neo-Marxism. In Richard H. Popkin, ed. *The ColumbiaHistory of Western Philosophy.* New York: MJF Books, 1999.

.Industry-Sponsored Research Biased?. Orange County [California] *Register.* January 22, 2003,News 11.

Jaki, Stanley L. .From Scientific Cosmology to a Created Universe. In Roy Abraham Varghese,ed., *The Intellectuals Speak Out About God.* Chicago: Regnery, 1984.

Jaki, Stanley L. .Science: Western or What?. *Intercollegiate Review* 26:1 (Fall 1990), pp. 3-12.

Johnson, Phillip E. *Darwin on Trial.* Washington, D.C.: Regnery, 1991.

Johnson, Phillip E. *Objections Sustained: Subversive Essays on Evolution, Law & Culture.* DownersGrove, IL: InterVarsity, 1998.

Johnson, Phillip E. .The Religion of the Blind Watchmaker. *Christian Leadership Ministries.* Retrieved from http://www.clm.org/real/ri9203/watchmkr.html.

Johnson, Phillip E. *The Right Questions: Truth, Meaning, and Public Debate.* Downers Grove, IL: Johnson, Phillip E. *The Wedge of Truth: Splitting the Foundations of Naturalism.* Downers Grove, IL:

Johnson, Samuel. .The Vision of Theodore, Hermit of Teneriffe. Retrieved from http://www.virtualsalt.com/lit/theodore.htm.

Jones, A. S. A. .The Games Skeptics Play. *Ex-Atheist.com.* Retrieved from http://www.exatheist.com/7.html.

Jones, Roger S. *Physics for the Rest of Us.* 1992. Reprint New York: Barnes and Noble, 1999.

Kearl, Michael. .Sociology of Knowledge. Retrieved from http://www.trinity.edu/~mkearl/knowledge.html.

Keas, Michael and Kerry Magruder. .Unified Studies Natural Science F-2002 Packet. OklahomaBaptist University, 2002. Retrieved from http://www.okbu.edu/academics/natsci/us/311/pack.pdf.

Kimball, Roger. *Tenured Radicals: How Politics Has Corrupted Our Higher Education*. Chicago: IvanR. Dee, 1998.

Knight, Robert H. *The Age of Consent: The Rise of Relativism and the Corruption of Popular Culture.*Dallas: Spence, 1998.

Kockelmans, Joseph J. .Continental Philosophy of Science. In Richard H. Popkin, ed. *TheColumbia History of Western Philosophy*. New York: MJF Books, 1999.

Kohm, Lynn Marie. .What is a Christian University? or How to Achieve Preeminence as aGraduate Institution. Retrieved online at <http://www.regent.edu/admin/cids/christianuniv.pdf>.

Kohn, Alexander. *False Prophets*. Rev. ed., New York: Barnes and Noble, 1988.

Kors, Alan Charles and Harvey A. Silverglate. *The Shadow University: The Betrayal of Liberty onAmerican Campuses*. New York: Harper Perennial, 1999.

Kreeft, Peter. *How to Win the Culture War*. Downers Grove, IL: InterVarsity, 2002.

Kuhn, Thomas S. *The Structure of Scientific Revolutions*. 2nd Ed. Chicago: University of Chicago,1970.

Lawler, Peter Augustine. .Conservative Postmodernism, Postmodern Conservatism. *Intercollegiate Review* 38:1 (Fall 2002), pp. 16-25.

Leo, John. .Gender Wars Redux. *U. S. News & World Report*, Feb. 27, 1999, 24.

Leo, John. .Nobel Prize for Fiction?. *U. S. News & World Report*, Jan. 25, 1999, 17.

Lunn, Arnold. *The Revolt Against Reason*. London: Eyre and Spottiswoode, 1950.

Macbeth, Norman. *Darwin Retried: An Appeal to Reason*. Ipswitch, MA: Gambit, 1971.

MacDougall, Curtis D. *Hoaxes*. 2nd Ed., New York: Dover, 1958.

McCallum, Dennis. *Christianity: The Faith that Makes Sense*. Wheaton: Tyndale House, 1992.

McCallum, Dennis, ed. *The Death of Truth*: Minneapolis: Bethany House, 1996.

McGrath, Alister. .The Christian Scholar in the 21ˢᵗ Century,. Christian Leadership Ministries. Retrieved from http://www.clm.org/real/ri0002/mcgrath.html.

Madison, G. B. .Hermeneutics: Gadamer and Ricoeur. In Richard H. Popkin, ed. *The ColumbiaHistory of Western Philosophy*. New York: MJF Books, 1999.

Makkreel, Rudolf A. .The Problem of Values in the Late Nineteenth Century. In Richard H.Popkin, ed. *The Columbia History of Western Philosophy*. New York: MJF Books, 1999.

Marsden, George. *The Outrageous Idea of Christian Scholarship*. New York: Oxford University Press,1997.

Marsden, George. .The State of Evangelical Christian Scholarship. *Reformed Journal* 37:9 (Sept.1987), pp. 12-16.

Martin, Jerry L. .Restoring American Cultural Institutions. *Society* 36:2 (Jan-Feb 1999), pp. 35-40.

May, Clifford D. .Chaos, Opportunity . . . and Caution in Africa. *Washington Times*. July 6, 2003.

Meyer, Stephen C. .The Origin of Life and the Death of Materialism. *Intercollegiate Review* 31:2(Spring 1996), pp. 24-43.

Milton, Richard. .The Open Society and Its Enemies. June 26, 2002.

<http://www.alternativescience.com/thes_and_Richard_ dawkins.htm>.

Minogue, Kenneth. ..Christophobia. and the West. *New Criterion* 21:10 (June 2003), pp. 4-13.

Moore, Thomas J. *Deadly Medicine: Why Tens of Thousands of Heart Patients Died in America.s WorstDrug Disaster.* New York: Simon and Schuster, 1995.

Moreland, J. P. .Academic Integration and the Christian Scholar. *The Real Issue.* Jan/Feb 2000, p.

Moreland, J. P. *Love Your God with All Your Mind: The Role of Reason in the Life of the Soul.* ColoradoSprings: Navpress, 1997.

Moreland, J. P. .Philosophical Apologetics, the Church, and Contemporary Culture. *Premise* 3:4(April 29, 1996), pp. 6ff. Retrieved from http://capo.org/premise/96/april/p960406. html.

.Piltdown Bird. *EXN.ca* Retrieved from http://exn.ca/ Templates/webisode.asp?story_id=2001033054.

Plantinga, Alvin. .Advice to Christian Philosophers. *Truth Journal.* Retrieved from http://www.leaderu.com/ truth/1truth10.html.

Plantinga, Alvin. .Darwin, Mind, and Meaning. Retrieved from UCSB Faculty-Staff ChristianFellowship, http://id-www.ucsb.edu/fscf/library/plantinga/dennett.html.

Plantinga, Alvin. .Methodological Naturalism? Part One: Is Science Religiously Neutral? ThreeExamples. The Faculty-Staff Christian Forum at the University of California at SantaBarbara. Retrieved from http://idwww.ucsb.edu/fscf/library/plantinga/mn/MN1.html.

Plantinga, Alvin. .On Christian Scholarship. The Faculty-Staff Christian Forum at the Universityof California at Santa Barbara. Retrieved from http://idwww.ucsb.edu/fscf/library/plantinga/OCS.html.

Plantinga, Alvin. .Theism, Atheism, and Rationality. *Truth Journal*. Retrieved fromhttp://www.leaderu.com/truth/3truth02.html.

.The Press Corps: Liberal, Liberal, Liberal. *Media Reality Check*. August 14, 2001. MediaResearchCenter.<http://www.mediaresearch.org/realitycheck/2001/20010814.asp>.

Preston, John, ed. *Paul K. Feyerabend: Knowledge, Science and Relativism*. Philsophical Papers,Volume 3. Cambridge: Cambridge University Press, 1999.

Rea, Michael C. *World Without Design: The Ontological Consequences of Naturalism*. New York:Oxford University Press, 2002.

Rector, Robert E., Kirk A. Johnson, and Lauren R. Noyes. .Sexually Active Teenagers Are MoreLikely to Be Depressed and to attempt Suicide. A Report to the Singer, Charles. *A History of Scientific Ideas*. 1959. Rpt., New York: Dorset, 1990.

Sloan, Christopher P. .Feathers for T. Rex? New Birdlike Fossils Are Missing Links in DinosaurEvolution. *National Geographic.* November 1999, pp. 98-107.

Sokal, Alan and Jean Bricmont. *Fashionable Nonsense: Postmodern Intellectuals. Abuse of Science.*New York: Picador USA, 1998.

Solzhenitsyn, Alexander. .A World Split Apart,. June 8, 1978. Retrieved from http://www.Columbia.edu/cu/Augustine/arch/Solzhenitsyn/harvard1978.html.

Sommers, Christina Hoff. *The War Against Boys: How Misguided Feminism Is Harming Our YoungMen.* New York: Simon & Schuster, 2000.

Sommers, Christina Hoff. *Who Stole Feminism?* New York: Simon and Schuster, 1994.

Sowell, Thomas. .Cultural Diversity: A World View. Retrieved from http://www.tsowell.com/spcultur.html.

Sowell, Thomas. .Morality Vs. Sanctimoniousness. Retrieved from http://www.tsowell.com/spmorali.html.

Stark, Rodney .False Conflict,. *The American Enterprise* 14:7 (Oct./Nov. 2003), pp. 27-33.

Stein, Harry. *How I Accidentally Joined the Vast Right-Wing Conspiracy (And Found Inner Peace).*New York: Delacorte, 2000.

Stolba, Christine. .Lying in a Room of One.s Own: How Women.s Studies Textbooks MiseducateStudents. *Independent Women.s Forum*, 2002. Retrieved from http://www.iwf.org/pdf/roomononesown.pdf.

Stoll, David. *Rigoberta Menchu and the Story of All Poor Guatemalans*. Boulder, CO: Westview, 1999.Stroll, Avrum. .Twentieth-Century Analytic Philosophy. In Richard H. Popkin, ed. *The Columbia History of Western Philosophy*. New York: MJF Books, 1999.

Wells, Jonathan. *Icons of Evolution: Science or Myth? Why Much of What We Teach About Evolution IsWrong*. Washington, D. C.: Regnery, 2000.

Whalen, David M. ..A Little More than Kin and Less than Kind.: The Affinity of Literature andPolitics. *Intercollegiate Review* 37:1 (Fall 2001), pp. 22-30.

Wieland, Carl. .National Geographic Backs Down. Sort Of. *Answers in Genesis*. Retrievedfromhttp://www.answersingenesis.org/docs2/4273news4-11-2999.asp?vPrint=1.

Wolterstorff, Nicholas. .The Mission of the Christian College at the End of the 20th Century. *Reformed Journal* 33:6 (June 1983), pp. 14-18.

Wolterstorff, Nicholas. *Reason Within the Bounds of Religion*. 2nd ed. Grand Rapids: Eerdmans,1984.

Xu Xing. .Feathers for T. Rex?. *National Geographic*, March 2000, n.p.

Zacharias, Ravi. *Jesus Among Other Gods: The Absolute Claims of the Christian Message.* Nashville:Word, 2000.

Zinsmeister, Karl. .The Shame of America.s One-Party Campuses. *The American Enterprise*, Sept.2002, 18-25.

Sykes, Charles J. *The Hollow Men: Politics and Corruption in Higher Education.* Washington, D.C:Regnery, 1990.

Torrey, E. Fuller. *Freudian Fraud: The Malignant Effect of Freud.s Theory on American Thought andCulture.* 1992. Rpt. New York: Harper, 1993.

Varghese, Roy Abraham. *The Intellectuals Speak Out About God.* Chicago: Regnery Gateway, 1984.Veith, Gene Edward Jr. *Postmodern Times: A Christian Guide to Contemporary Thought and Culture.*

Wheaton, IL: Crossway Books, 1994.Vitz, Paul C. *Faith of the Fatherless: The Psychology of Atheism.* Dallas: Spence Publishing, 1999.

Wells, Jonathan. .Catch-23. *Center for Science and Culture.* July 1, 2002. Retrieved fromhttp://www.discovery.org.

Wells, Jonathan. .Critics Rave Over Icons of Evolution: A Response to Published Reviews. Center for Science and Culture, June 12, 2002. Retrieved from http://www.discovery.org.

Heritage Center for DataAnalysis. *The Heritage Foundation.* June 2, 2002. Retrieved fromhttp://www.heritage.org/ Research/Family/cda0304.cfm.

Roberts, J. M. *Twentieth Century: The History of the World, 1901 to 2000.* New York: Viking, 1999.

Rockmore, Tom. .Karl Marx. In Richard H. Popkin, ed. *The Columbia History of WesternPhilosophy.* New York: MJF Books, 1999.

Romey, William D. .Science as Fiction or Nonfiction?: A Physical Scientist.s View from a GeneralSemantics Perspective. *Et Cetera* 37:3 (Fall 1980), pp. 201-207.

Rudel, Thomas K. and Judith M. Gerson. .Postmodernism, Institutional Change, and Academic

Workers: A Sociology of Knowledge. *Social Science Quarterly* 80:2 (June 1999), pp. 213ff.

Sandage, Allan. .A Scientist Reflects on Religious Belief. *Truth Journal.* Retrieved fromhttp://www.leaderu.com/ truth/1truth15.html.

Schlafly, Phyllis. *Feminist Fantasies.* Dallas: Spence Publishing, 2003.

Freeman, Derek. *The Fateful Hoaxing of Margaret Mead: A Historical Analysis of Her Samoan Research.*Boulder, CO: Westview, 1999.

Gangel, Kenneth O. .Integrating Faith and Learning: Principles and Process. *Bibliotheca Sacra*,April-June, 1978. Retrieved online at <http://www.ici.edu/journals/bibsac/7584/78b1.htm>.

Genetics: Readings from Scientific American, With Introductions by Cedric I. Davern. San Francisco: W.H. Freeman, 1981.

Childers, Jeff. .Chapter 5 Summary, .Christian Scholarship Symposium at ACU on *TheOutrageous Idea of Christian Scholarship* by George Marsden... Abilene ChristianUniversity, Feb. 1999. Retrieved from http://www.acu.edu/academics/adamscenter/resources/faithlearning/christianschool.html.

.Christophobia. Retrieved from http://home.infostations.com/quietsun/athart6.htm.

Clark, Thomas W. .Humanism and Postmodernism: A Reconciliation. *The Humanist*, Jan-Feb1993, pp. 18-23.

Cremo, Michael A. and Richard L. Thompson. *Forbidden Archeology: The Hidden History of theHuman Race*. Rev. Ed., Los Angeles: Bhaktivedanta Book Publishing, 1998.

Cremo, Michael. *Forbidden Archeology.s Impact*, 2nd. ed. Los Angeles: Bhaktivedanta, 2001.

Crews, Frederick C., ed. *Unauthorized Freud: Doubters Confront a Legend*. New York: Viking, 1998.

Culverwell, Nathaniel. *An Elegant and Learned Discourse of the Light of Nature* [1652]. Ed. Robert A.Greene and Hugh MacCallum. Toronto: University of Toronto, 1971.

Curtler, Hugh Mercer. The Myopia of the Cultural Relativist. *The Intercollegiate Review* 38:1 (Fall2002), pp. 35-43.

Custred, Glynn. The Forbidden Discovery of Kennewick Man. *Academic Questions.* 13:3Summer 2000, pp. 12-30.

Darwin, Francis, ed. *The Life and Letters of Charles Darwin.* New York: D. Appleton, 1888.

GOD IS YOUR DAILY FOCUS.

GOD IS YOUR ULTIMATE VISION.

ABOUT AUTHOR

Biswajit Pattajoshi has served as author and teacher for over a decade. He received God's touch and words in 2001, an experience which revolutionised his outreach and intimate connection with God, and receiving subsequent baptism. He has travelled extensively and spreads the message of God's love, healing and power and glory to people of all nations. He leads a humble life and loves to diligently serve the lord and service to mankind. He lives in India.

Printed in the United States
By Bookmasters